GW00640849

Robyn Wilson is a journalist turned restaurateuse. Born in New Zealand (where she caught her first fish at the age of seven), she studied modern languages at Auckland University before joining the *Weekly News* as a trainee journalist. She then worked in Spain, Mexico, South Africa and the United Kingdom on newspapers, magazines and in television. Since settling in the United Kingdom in 1977 she has written for a variety of publications including the *Financial Times*, the *Sunday Times*, and *TV Times*.

In December 1983 she opened a restaurant in London's Hatton Garden, working closely with her two French chefs on the creation of menus. With her executive chef, Dominique Cure, she visits Billingsgate Fish Market to select the daily Fish Specials. It was these dawn visits to Billingsgate that really got her hooked. She now cooks and eats little else but fish.

ROBYN WILSON

FISH

SPHERE BOOKS LIMITED

To Joyce Mullis,
who showed us how to fillet a whitebait

SPHERE BOOKS LTD

Published by the Penguin Group
27 Wrights Lane, London W8 5TZ, England
Viking Penguin Inc., 40 West 23rd Street, New York, New York 10010, USA
Penguin Books Australia Ltd, Ringwood, Victoria, Australia
Penguin Books Canada Ltd, 2801 John Street, Markham, Ontario, Canada L3R 1B4
Penguin Books (NZ) Ltd, 182–190 Wairau Road, Auckland 10, New Zealand

Penguin Books Ltd, Registered Offices: Harmondsworth, Middlesex, England

First published in paperback in Great Britain by Sphere Books Ltd 1988

Copyright © by Robyn Wilson 1988
Line drawings copyright © by Malcolm Lauder 1988 and by courtesy of
Café Fish des Amis du Vin

Printed and bound in Great Britain by
Richard Clay Ltd, Bungay, Suffolk
Set in 11 on 12½ pt Monophoto Sabon

Except in the United States of America, this book is sold subject
to the condition that it shall not, by way of trade or otherwise, be lent,
re-sold, hired out, or otherwise circulated without the
publisher's prior consent in any form of binding or cover other than
that in which it is published and without a similar condition
including this condition being imposed on the subsequent purchaser

INTRODUCTION

Fish and your health

Fish is the healthiest protein food that you can eat. Just *two* meals of fish a week can *halve* your chances of ever having a heart attack. The Eskimos of Northern Greenland and the Japanese have the lowest incidence of heart disease in the world – and it's all due to the fish they eat ... or, more precisely, the oil in that fish. Fish oil contains a unique substance called **Omega 3**, which actually breaks down the cholesterol which clogs up your arteries, causing blood clots and heart attacks.

Over the last three years I have talked to doctors, research scientists and nutritionists on three continents, and, without exception, they have agreed on one thing: by eating only two meals of fish a week (one of those using preferably an oily fish like sardine, salmon, or mackerel, which are all high in Omega 3) you can not only halve your chances of a heart attack, but also significantly increase your resistance to a number of other diseases, including arthritis, migraine headaches, multiple sclerosis, eczema and breast cancer.

The evidence is incontrovertible. The Eskimos of Northern Greenland live on a diet that we would condemn as unbalanced and unhealthy: no fresh fruit and vegetables, no added fibre. They seem to survive exclusively on fish with the odd meal of whale or seal for special occasions. Yet the incidence of heart diseases there is ten times lower than it is in the United Kingdom.

Two Danish doctors, Jorn Dyerberg and Helmut Bang, conducted a study over a period of ten years in the region of Igdlorssuit, on the northern coast of Greenland. Records for the region's two thousand inhabitants show that in that ten years there was not one recorded incident of a heart attack. Careful analysis of the Eskimos' lifestyle and environment proved that the absence of heart disease was entirely due to the Eskimo diet: fish, fish and more fish.

In 1960 in Holland, Dr Kromhout of the University of Leiden, made a similar connection between a fish-rich diet and a reduced level of heart disease. He began monitoring the diets of a sample group of eight hundred and fifty-two middle-aged men in the town of Zutphen. Some ate fish twice a week, some ate more, some ate none. Twenty years later he concluded his study and fed his data into the University computer. The results confirmed his theory. The men of Zutphen who consumed an average of thirty grams of fish a day (just over an ounce a day, or the equivalent of two four ounce portions a week) were less than half as likely to suffer from heart disease as those who ate no fish.

If you're still not convinced, take at look at recent figures from the northern coast of Japan, where they eat almost half a pound (two hundred grams), of fish a day. Not only is their incidence of heart disease less than a fifth of ours, but they also live longer than any other group on earth.

Three very different communities – the Eskimos of Greenland, the Dutch burghers of Zutphen and the fisherfolk of Northern Japan – with one thing in common: a regular intake of fish oil. And fish oil, as Doctors Dyerberg, Bang and Kromhout discovered, is very high in Poly Unsaturated Fatty Acids, or **PUFAs** for short. These are not the same Poly Unsaturated Fatty Acids that are found in vegetable oils, but distinctive **N-3 PUFAs**, so called because they have a special 'double bond' on the third link of the molecular chain. Vegetable oil PUFAs have their double bond on the sixth link and therefore have none of the uniquely beneficial properties of the N-3 PUFAs found in fish oils. In the US, to avoid PUFA confusion, the N-3 PUFA is now known as Omega 3.

All fish, shellfish and crustaceans contain Omega 3 – though some contain considerably more than others – which works to prevent heart disease in several different ways: Firstly, it lowers the 'triglyceride' or blood fat levels in the bloodstream. This prevents a build-up of fatty deposits on the walls of the arteries, and therefore helps the blood to flow more freely. Secondly, it works on the blood's clotting mechanism, the platelets. Omega 3 makes the platelets less likely to cluster together and form a clot or thrombosis which could block the artery, prevent the blood getting through and cause a heart attack. The combination of artery walls clogged with fatty deposits plus a blood clot blocking the blood's passage is the most common cause of a heart attack. Thirdly, Omega 3 works on the red blood cells giving you thinner, faster-flowing blood. Finally, and most importantly, Omega 3 actually works to reduce existing cholesterol levels in your bloodstream. We all need some cholesterol – but too much can be fatal. Like the triglycerides, it builds up on the artery walls and clogs up the arteries. If, over a period of years, you have consumed too much cholesterol by over-dosing on fatty meats, butter and other saturated fats, the polyunsaturated fatty acids of Omega 3 can cut that cholesterol down.

Research currently being carried out in the United States suggests that you may even be able to do that in the very same meal. Tests on rats show that Omega 3 consumed at the same time as high cholesterol foods significantly affected cholesterol intake.

So far no long-term tests have been done on humans but Dr Marian Childs of the University of Washington in Seattle has had well-documented success with her tests on rats. Dr Childs has been able to inhibit the absorption of cholesterol eaten in the same meal by rats who were fed oysters and clams. Dr Childs may well be able to prove that it is okay (as far as your heart is concerned) to indulge in the odd high cholesterol cream cake, provided you pay penance with an oyster or two immediately before or after. However this is *not* a green light for dieters: Omega 3 does not alter the calorie count.

A further piece of heartening information on the Omega 3 front is that Omega 3 appears to play a curative role as well as a protective one in the battle against heart disease. For a period of eight months, American researcher Dr Bonnie Weiner fed fish oil to seven pigs in whom coronary artery disease had been induced. A control group of eleven pigs, similarly afflicted with heart disease, were given no fish oil. Dr Weiner's tests proved conclusively that the daily supplement of Omega 3 significantly retarded the development of the coronary artery disease in those seven pigs.

While Omega 3 is being hailed as possibly the most important nutritional 'discovery' this century in the quest for healthier hearts, doctors on both sides of the Atlantic are now convinced that it plays a much wider protective role. They believe Omega 3 to have therapeutic effects on a whole range of other diseases, from arthritis and asthma to breast cancer, kidney disease and migraines.

According to Dr Alexander Leaf of the Department of Preventative Medicine at the Harvard Medical School, a world authority on the benefits of a fish-rich diet, there is evidence to show that Omega 3 can reduce or ameliorate:

- Rheumatoid arthritis: Omega 3 may encourage the blood to produce prostaglandins which ease the inflammation of arthritic joints.

- Migraines: Omega 3 is believed to reduce the amount of serotonin in the bloodstream. Serotonin is the chemical which causes blood vessels to contract during a migraine attack, making it difficult for the blood to get through. I used to get a migraine attack about once a month. Since I started eating fish three or four times a week, the frequency of my migraine headaches has reduced dramatically – to two or three a year. This is difficult to interpret as coincidence.

- Asthma: In tests in the United States, Omega 3 has shown to be beneficial in ameliorating the effects of auto-immune diseases, such as asthma.

- Breast Cancer: Work being done by Dr Rashida Karmali of Rutgers University New Jersey indicates that Omega 3 may inhibit the growth of certain tumours. Research being done here in the United Kingdom also indicates that dietary fat may be a primary cause of breast cancer – and Omega 3 is known to counteract some dietary fats.

- Kidney Disease: According to Dr Leaf, work being done on 'nude mice' (the species is totally hairless) with congenital kidney disease has indicated that regular addition of Omega 3 to the diet can reverse certain kidney conditions. In the 'nude mice' tests the researchers had a one hundred per cent success rate.

However, even the most committed of the fish oil researchers suggest we take some of the 'miracle fish cure' tales with a modicum of caution. One new report even suggests that regular doses of Omega 3 can delay the effects of aging and promote longevity. This is based on evidence that the northern Japanese and the Icelandic, who have extremely fish-rich diets, live longer than anyone else. But, like many 'fish is a miracle food' claims, this longevity thesis lacks sufficient documentation *yet* to be written into the text books.

Like most of his colleagues working with fish oils in Harvard's Preventitive Medicine Department, Dr Leaf is 'excited, enthusiastic – but very cautious' about the myriad claims that are surfacing about the benefits of fish oils. 'What we do know for certain,' says Alex Leaf, 'is that even one ounce of fish a day can halve the morbidity rate from heart disease.'

You don't have to have your ounce of fish on a daily basis – four ounces twice a week should be sufficient to keep your Omega 3 levels up. All fish contains some Omega 3, but oily fish such as mackerel, sardines, and salmon contain much more than lean fish like cod, plaice and sole. A healthy diet should, say the US fish nutrition experts, include a four ounce serving of an oily fish once a week. In the alphabetical fish guide, fish high in Omega 3 are marked with an ⬚O⬚ .

Fish and your figure

Not only is fish incredibly good for your health, it is also the least fattening protein food that you can eat. Four ounces (one hundred grams) of white fish – hake, haddock or even cod – contains about 85 calories. That's less than a boiled egg, only half as much as a piece of grilled chicken, less than a third as many calories as the same sized piece of beef, and about a fifth of the calories in a four ounce (one hundred gram) slice of cheddar cheese. Weight for weight, there's nothing on the protein front to match it.

The chart overleaf gives you the calorie counts of a sample range of fish comparing them with similarly-sized portions of other foods you are likely to eat. The calorie value of almost a hundred different fish, shellfish and crustaceans is given in the Fish A–Z.

Just as important as which fish you eat, is the manner in which you cook it. A 4 oz (100 g) cod fillet, steamed, grilled or poached, will clock up about 85 calories on the calorie counter. That same piece of cod dipped in batter and crisply fried to golden perfection will cost your body about 215 calories, more than two and a half times as much. Fish wrapped in batter and deep-fried is on the no-no list on two counts: it is loaded with surplus calories, and the oil that fish is fried in is generally high in very harmful saturated fats.

One of the great attractions of fish for weight-watchers is that it can be cooked quickly and simply – without lots of added extras adding lots of extra calories. In fact, by just adding five items to your lean fish fillet, all of them virtually calorie-free, you can prepare yourself a fish dish in fifteen minutes. Those five items are:

1 A piece of tin foil.
2 The juice of half a fresh lime or lemon.
3 A heaped tablespoon of fresh chopped herbs (basil, tarragon, chervil, mint, or even parsley)
4 Salt.
5 Freshly-ground black pepper.

Instructions for cooking with foil are in the A–Z.

Calorie comparisons

approx per
4 oz (100 g)
portion raw

84	Cod
84	Hake
86	Plaice
96	Lemon Sole
200	Mackerel
98	Monkfish
170	Salmon (varies seasonally)
100	Whiting
120	Prawns (meat only)
84	Crab (meat only)
54	Cockles
56	Oysters
80	Scallops
150	Chicken (skinless)
200	Lamb (lean)
180	Beef (lean)
90	Egg (size 2, boiled)
450	Cheddar Cheese
350	Brie
105	Butter (1 level tablespoon)
120	Olive Oil (1 tablespoon)
98	Potato (baked)
16	Tomato
70	Bread (1 oz slice, wholemeal)
75	Wine (4 oz glass, dry red or white)

Fish and your sex life

Fish not only makes you look good – it makes you feel good too; mostly because of the mineral content. That tale about oysters being good for your love life is actually true, because oysters contain a very high proportion of zinc and selenium, both minerals that affect potency, fertility and what one American expert calls 'amatory prowess'.

When that legendary Latin lover Casanova downed fifty oysters a night to maintain his stamina, he was probably just counteracting a zinc deficiency.

MINERALS

Fish and shellfish are an almost unsurpassed source of most of the important minerals your body needs. Some shellfish, such as oysters, mussels and whelks, provide up to eight times the amount of vital minerals that meat does. The main minerals that seafood can provide are:

Zinc

This is where that story about oysters being good for your love life comes from. Oysters have eight times as much zinc as fillet steak, and zinc is the mineral that most experts in this field claim can improve your sex drive. A six month study carried out in Michigan in the United States on a group of male hospital patients showed that a dramatic increasing in their zinc intake equated with an equally significant increase not just in their libido (sexual urges) but in potency and fertility levels.

In his book *Sexual Nutrition*, America's Dr Morton Walker claims that it is not just the zinc, but zinc plus selenium that gives oyster eaters increased libido and greater stamina. Anthropology students may be interested to know that Pacific oysters have twice as much zinc as Atlantic oysters.

Selenium
As well as aiding what Dr Walker calls your 'amatory prowess', selenium is also believed to play a role in preventing the growth of some cancers, by stimulating the body's immune system.

Phosphorus
Fish and shellfish are rich in phosphorus, the mineral which, as well as aiding bone construction, is reputed to improve your cerebral functions – which is why so many people talk about fish as 'brain food'.

Potassium
Many white fish, including cod and flounder are high in potassium which helps regulate blood pressure and can lower high pressure.

Calcium
Small fish such as sardines can be an important source of calcium, now regarded as critical in the fight against osteoporosis, which causes brittle bones in older people and particularly in women. Calcium also helps strengthen your fingernails.

Iodine
Seafood provides an almost unrivalled source of iodine, the mineral which influences the activity of the thyroid gland and thus controls body metabolism. A deficiency of iodine can lead to mental retardation. There is no evidence yet to prove the reverse is true but this could be another reason why fish is so widely held to be good for the brain.

VITAMINS
Fish can also supply most of your daily vitamins, with the exception of Vitamin C. It is a particularly good source of Vitamins A and D. Vitamin D is an important bone builder,

and Vitamin A has long been known as one of the beauty vitamins because of its work in keeping skin supple. Vitamin A is also believed to improve your sight. The other beauty vitamin, E, is present in most oily fish.

Fish is also an excellent source of all the major B vitamins, including: Thiamin-B1, needed for the nervous system; Riboflavin-B2, which aids body metabolism; Pyrodoxine-B6, which many women now take as a supplement to counteract the effects of pre-menstrual tension; B12 and B15, which are both thought to be excellent hangover relievers; and Niacin, which is active in releasing body energy. The B-group vitamins are important for overall body tone and healthy, shiny hair.

No wonder the *Chicago Herald Tribune* ran a headline proclaiming: Fish the Miracle Food! It sounds like an ad man's dream product. All these amazing health benefits, as well as promising the user a sylph-like figure – and an increased libido! All from eating fish!

Well, with all this going for fish, why don't we eat more of it? Research conducted by Fish Marketing Authorities all round the world has come up with a number of reasons why so many people are so resistant to eating fish. They can be summed up in about 3 points:

1 Too many bones.
2 Too difficult to prepare.
3 Too boring.

The following very simple guide should tell you almost everything you need to know about the enormous variety of fish and shellfish that is available in the United Kingdom, including how to prepare them, how to cook them – and how to get the bones out. Listed alphabetically, there are dozens of helpful hints from the best way to choose fish (look into its eyes – they should be clear and shiny), to the simplest way of cleaning fish (cover your fingers with salt, that way you won't lose it), to the easiest way to poach a salmon (pop it inside a pair of tights).

The guide also lists, for most fish, the calories contained in a 4 oz (100 g) portion, and whether a fish is lean and low-calorie, or oily. The oily ones may be higher in calories but they are the ones with the most Omega 3. For a really healthy heart you should have at least one meal of oily fish such as salmon, trout, tuna, sardines, or herrings a week. The cooking suggestions that follow most fish listings have been gathered not just from the traditional fish cooking regions of Europe but from chefs in the United States, Australia and New Zealand as well. You may decide that mint is not the flavour you would choose to enhance a trout –but you won't know until you try it!

Symbols
Fish and fish cookery terms are listed alphabetically. Where fish are listed, the French name is generally given, and where possible the number of calories contained in a 4 oz (100 g) raw portion. For vegetables, herbs and spices, the calorie count also relates to a 4 oz (100 g) portion. For alcohol and spirits, the calorie count relates to a 1 fl oz (25 ml) portion.

The symbol $\boxed{L}$ means the fish is low in fat; the symbol $\boxed{O}$ indicates the fish is particularly high in Omega 3. The term round or flat describes the shape of fish and thus the way it should be filleted. A heart shape $\boxed{\heartsuit}$ suggests that the fish or shellfish may have properties which some doctors believe could improve your sex life. $\boxed{HC}$ indicates a generally high calorie content, and $\boxed{LC}$ indicates a generally low calorie content.

If a fish or a fish cookery term is printed in bold it will appear under that alphabetical listing.

Measures (approximate equivalents)

Solid Measurements

1 lb (16 oz)	400 grams
½ lb (8 oz)	200 grams
¼ lb (4 oz)	100 grams
1 oz	25 grams

1 kilo (1000 grams)	2 lb 3 oz
½ kilo (500 grams)	1 lb 1½ oz
100 grams	3½ oz

Solid Equivalents

1 oz butter	approx 2 level tablespoons
1 oz flour	approx 4 level tablespoons

Liquid Measurements

1 quart	1.1 litres
1 pint	6 dl (600 ml)
½ pint	3 dl (300 ml)
¼ pint	1.5 dl (150 ml)
1 tablespoon	15 ml
1 dessertspoon	10 ml
1 teaspoon	5 ml
1 cup (approx)	½ pint = 300 ml
1 cup (approx)	16 tablespoons

Oven Temperature Approx. Equivalents

250 F	120 C	Gas Mark ½	Very Slow
350 F	175 C	Gas Mark 3	Moderate
400 F	205 C	Gas Mark 6	Moderately Hot
450 F	230 C	Gas Mark 8	Hot
475 F	245 C	Gas Mark 9	Very Hot

Abalone ♡ L 110 ormeau/shellfish

A marine snail shaped rather like a large ear which is highly prized by the French for its delicate taste and by some orientals for its alleged aphrodisiac properties. Also known as the ormer, it is particularly popular in the Channel Islands (for the taste, not the other things, claim the Jersey folk) where its harvest is now restricted to 'Spring' tides occurring in those months with an 'R' in them – September through to April. In California, where it is held in even higher regard as a gourmet treat, it is also on the restricted list and only abalone over seven inches in diameter may be removed from the rocks. It is now illegal to ship Californian abalone outside their home state, such is the paucity of the crop.

Abalone is something of an acquired taste – it can be very tough and very chewy unless it is expertly handled. The meat from the abalone's muscular foot, with which it clings to submerged rocks, must be beaten hard with a wooden mallet for at least 1 minute to tenderise it, or it is inedible. Once beaten, it is either cut into small steaks and fried very quickly in a little butter – no more than a minute on each side; or stewed slowly with onions, carrots, celery, garlic, a bay leaf and a half bottle of Muscadet for several hours. Some Channel Islands connoisseurs will leave their ormers simmering overnight. Here is a good basic recipe: *Take 1½ lbs (600 g) of ormer steaks, which have been well-beaten with a mallet or rolling pin, and arrange in layers in a casserole, dotting each layer with about 4 oz (100 g) of butter cut into small pieces, 1 medium chopped onion, 1 finely chopped garlic clove and 1 heaped tablespoon of chopped parsley. Add 2 cloves, a bouquet garni and ½ pint (3 dl) Muscadet. Bring to the boil and simmer for about 30 minutes or until the fish is tender. Remove the ormers and keep them warm. Strain the liquid, then stir in small pieces of* **beurre manié** *until the sauce thickens, making sure it does not boil. Pour sauce over the ormers, and serve garnished with chopped parsley.*

Abalone is also highly prized in Japan where it is eaten raw as **sushi** and in Australia where it is marinated in oil and lemon and sliced on a salad. In the UK, abalone can be found in cans in oriental food stores, and some of the better delicatessens. If you do acquire a tin of abalone, don't bother about the wooden mallet – tinned abalone has already been beaten.

Aïoli   HC

A creamy garlic mayonnaise that can be served as a dip for cold prawns or a sauce for cold poached fish. In Provence they serve it with hot boiled salt cod. It is also a perfect dip for **crudités**. *Mix 4 large cloves of garlic, ground finely in a mortar or mixer, with a pinch of salt, ½ teaspoon of lemon juice and the yolk of 1 large egg, then, still stirring, or blending in the mixer – add ½ pint (3 dl) of good olive oil, drop by drop at first, then in a continuous stream, until blended. If the mixture is too thick, thin it with a little* *white wine mixed with an equal quantity of warm water until it is the right consistency.*

Slimmers should note that a 4 oz (100 g) portion of Aïoli is about 820 calories, 1 teaspoon is about 40 calories. You could halve that by making your Aïoli from finely ground garlic and a little white wine mixed into one of the low-calorie mayonnaises available in most supermarkets.

Alcohol

A dash of alcohol splashed on to a fillet wrapped in foil, or added to a sauce can make all the difference to a fish dish – without making too much difference to the calorie count. A tablespoon of dry wine (white or red) will add only 10 calories, a tablespoon of Pernod adds about 35 calories, calvados – 30, brandy – 25. Alcohol added to a recipe before cooking will not have any effect on your faculties: all the alcohol is burned off during cooking leaving only the taste behind.

Serious calorie counters should remind themselves that a generous 5 oz (125 g) glass of dry wine, red, white or rosé, is about 90 calories; not much more than a slice of whole-meal bread. If you have to choose, remember that the wine will do nothing for your fibre intake but an awful lot for your morale, especially if you are at the difficult stage of your diet. It could also benefit your health: in New York some doctors claim that a small amount of wine is beneficial in that it eases hypertension. One New York State hospital now prescribes a glass of wine with the evening meal: they say it works better than sleeping pills in aiding relaxation.

Almond   HC   640

The nut that traditionally appears atop a trout turned golden brown in a generous portion of butter, known as either Truite Aux Amandes or Truite Amandine. A slightly healthier alternative is to make an almond **butter** from ground almonds and a little softened butter. Serve the trout topped with a slim circular slice of the almond butter garnished with a sprinkling of chopped almonds and a sprig of dill or parsley. A ten-pence-piece-size slice of almond butter will set you back about 50 calories – rather than 200 for the traditional almonds browned in butter. Almonds go surprisingly well with crustacea and shellfish – try putting them with crab, grapefruit segments and mayonnaise. Or mix them into a salad with smoked eel, celery, orange slices, spring onions and spinach leaves.

To skin almonds: blanch them in boiling water for a few seconds then rub the skins off while they are still warm.

Anchoiade   HC

An anchovy and garlic paste that can be used spread on toast – or even better, on brioche – as a snack, starter or canapé. High in calories, but you need very little. *Take a 2 oz (50 g) tin of anchovies, drain, then soak the fish in a little wine or milk for a few minutes to remove any excess saltiness (only if you find anchovies too salty for your taste). Mash them up with 2 finely ground cloves of garlic, 1 teaspoon of lemon juice, a little black pepper and 4 tablespoons olive oil. Toast triangles of bread on one side, spread the anchovy mixture on the untoasted side, sprinkle with a little finely chopped onion and parsley and place under hot grill for about 1 minute.*

Anchovy   O   170 anchois/round

Anchovies in their natural state are not great travellers so you will rarely find fresh anchovies in the UK. They are one of the treats of a Mediterranean summer holiday, dark, greeny-blue with sparkling silver bellies, never more than about six inches in length. You are supposed to be able to tell an anchovy from a sardine by its protruding upper jaw, large eyes and disproportionately wide mouth. Like sardines, fresh anchovies are at their best plain grilled, served with lemon and freshly ground black pepper. Or try them Sardinian-style, boned and stuffed with a thin slice of cheese.

Away from the Mediterranean you are more likely to encounter them filleted and packed in tins of oil or brine. Tinned anchovies are usually preserved with salt – lots of it. You can remove some of that salt by soaking the anchovy fillets in a little milk or white wine for a few minutes, but the essence of the anchovy is its very piquant taste. Anchovies are comparatively high in calories but, because of their strong flavour, you need use only a very small amount. They can be used in a **sauce** to perk up a bland fish dish; in **Anchoiade**, a garlic and anchovy savoury topping for toast; in **Tapenade**, an olive and anchovy spread; or in **Bagna Cauda**, which is a delectable but calorific Mediterranean mixture of olive oil, garlic and anchovies served hot as a dip for raw vegetables. Anchovies are a useful and lively addition to **stuffings** for fish that might otherwise be a little dull, for instance, combined with olives and breadcrumbs in a stuffing for **squid**.

Angler-fish

See **monkfish**.

Anise   65

A plant with a licorice-like taste, whose seed is used to

flavour liqueurs like Pernod, Ricard and pastis. Used in moderation, for they have quite a marked flavour, these anise-based liqueurs give a marvellous lift to fish and shellfish dishes.

You can make a Pernod **butter** with softened butter, shallots and Pernod to garnish plain grilled fish. Or try flambéed scallops in Pernod: *Sauté scallops over a very high heat in a little butter with some chopped spring onions and seasoning for about 2–3 minutes then pour a slug (a good tablespoon for every two servings) of warmed Pernod into a serving ladle. Add a match to this so that it flames in the ladle, and pour – still flaming – into the scallops. Stir the scallops around in it quickly for less than a minute, then place the warm scallops on a bed of salad. You can pour over the pan juices as they are or you can add a little cream to the juices while they are still in the pan, heat gently and pour this over the scallops.* If you are not a Pernod drinker but want to experiment with Pernod recipes, buy a miniature rather than a whole bottle.

Aphrodisiac

The Russians have long believed that caviar is an aphrodisiac, and **oysters** are believed by many to have aphrodisiac qualities. Dr Morton Walker in his book, *Sexual Nutrition*, claims it is the minerals zinc and selenium in the oysters that aid 'amatory prowess'. If this theory is true then perhaps the **cockle** and the **whelk** deserve greater recognition.

Aspic

A clear jelly made from fish stock – usually the liquid that the fish to be coated in aspic has been poached in – plus gelatine, wine and egg whites. A whole fish, especially a

Those alleged aphrodisiacs:

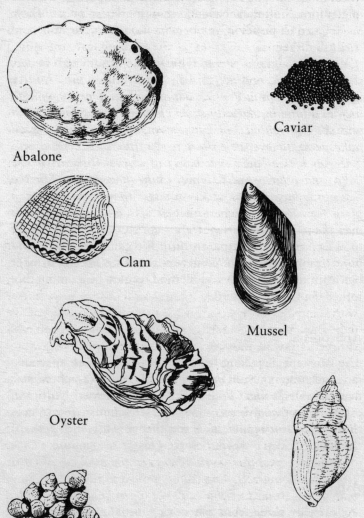

Abalone

Caviar

Clam

Mussel

Oyster

Whelk

Winkles

trout or salmon, coated in aspic makes an impressive centre-piece for a buffet luncheon or supper: *After poaching the fish in a* **court-bouillon**, *remove the fish, strain the remaining stock and* **reduce** *to ½ pint (3 dl) by boiling hard. Add ¼ pint (1.5 dl) of white wine, the whites of 2 eggs well-beaten, a finely crushed eggshell, and a ¼ oz (6 g) of gelatine. Simmer gently for 5 minutes, then allow to stand for 10 minutes before skimming all the bits and pieces off the surface. Decorate the fish with cucumber, carrots, peppers or whatever takes your fancy (stick them to the fish with a little aspic jelly) then pour over a covering of aspic. If it starts to set before you have finished decorating, place your bowl of aspic in a larger bowl of warm water to melt it slightly.*

In New Zealand, where they are always coming up with new things to do with **trout**, they use rosé wine in the court-bouillon and in the aspic to turn cold poached trout into a pretty pink party piece. Whitebait are also attractive in aspic, with lemon juice, tabasco, gelatine, water, wine and a dash of cream. Or make a highly impressive (but very easy) starter with Timbales of Seafood in a Muscadet Jelly – attractive individual moulds shaped like large thimbles, filled with shrimps, prawns, mussels, cockles and **julienned** vegetables in a Muscadet aspic, made from the shellfish stock, Muscadet and gelatine: *If you don't have thimble-shaped moulds, round ramekins will be just as effective. Warm ½ pint (3 dl) of Muscadet and dissolve 4 leaves of gelatine in it. Pour a little into each mould, then line the moulds with strips of smoked salmon – about 1 oz (25 g) per mould. Then, dividing the quantities evenly between the moulds, add 4 oz (100 g) fresh mussels, 4 oz (100 g) peeled prawns, 2 oz (50 g) baby clams (tinned, if you can't get fresh), and 2 hard boiled eggs, thinly sliced. Add the rest of the Muscadet jelly, and refrigerate to set. Remove from moulds carefully and serve, smoked salmon side up, on a bed of lemon and lime* **sauce**.

To make the sauce: Place 2 tablespoons sugar, the juice of 4 large lemons, and the juice of 4 limes in a small pan. Reduce till it is nearly caramelized, then add ¼ pint (1.5 dl) strong chicken stock or fish **fumet**. Reduce this by half, until the sauce is of a thick consistency, then remove from the heat and cool. Garnish the timbales with a sprig of fresh tarragon or chervil.

Au Bleu

A method of cooking fish – especially fresh water fish – that have reached you live, or have been dead for a very short time so that they are still coated with their natural slime. This mucous will produce a blue tinge in cooking. If the fish is still alive, kill it with a firm blow to the head, remove gills and fins and gut quickly. Do not scale or you may lose the 'slime'. Sprinkle with warm vinegar, then plunge the fish into a **court-bouillon** and simmer till cooked, depending on size (see **Canadian Theory**). Serve hot or cold with sauce – perhaps **Hollandaise** or **Gribiche**. Truite Au Bleu is probably the most common Au Bleu dish.

Aubergine   16

Also known as the eggplant on account of the shape and colour of one member of the species, which is small, white and ovoid. The most common is the deep purple aubergine, which is not often used with fish but makes an occasional appearance in a sauce to perk up a plain white fish, as in this American recipe for Sautéed Fish with Eggplant or Aubergine: Peel and dice a medium-sized aubergine and sprinkle with salt then leave to sweat off its bitter juices for half an hour. Rinse and dry well. Heat 2 tablespoons oil in a pan, cook gently 1 chopped medium-sized onion until translucent, then add the aubergine. Cook for further 5

minutes, then add 3 large chopped and peeled tomatoes plus
½ teaspoon tarragon and simmer until the eggplant is very
soft. Season with salt and pepper. Keep warm.

Meanwhile cut 1½ lbs (600 g) of plain white fish fillets
into serving size pieces – cod or whiting or any of the
freshwater fish like roach – dust with seasoned flour and
cook very quickly in 2 tablespoons oil which has been pre-
heated with 2 tablespoons butter. The principle of sautéeing
is to have the oil and butter very hot so that the flavour and
juices of the fish are immediately sealed in. Cook according
to the **Canadian Theory** *and drain well so that the fish is*
not soggy or oily. Place pools of the aubergine mixture on
individual plates, serve the fish in the centre and sprinkle
with fresh chopped parsley.

Aubergines are low in calories when raw – only 4 calories
per 1 oz (25 g) – but beware – they do absorb any oil they are
cooked in.

Avocado   252

An avocado sliced into crescents, decorated with crab meat,
topped with a dressing that is half mayonnaise (low-cal if
you're weight-watching), half yoghurt (Greek cows' yoghurt
tastes best because it is creamier than most), with a dash of
fresh lime juice and a little white wine, garnished with a few
chopped fresh coriander leaves, makes a simple but effective
starter. Avocado is very high in calories (a whole avocado is
getting on for 500 calories), but slice it into crescents and
serve with crab and you will only need a quarter of an
avocado per person.

Puréed and added to either real **mayonnaise** or low-cal
mayonnaise together with a little lemon juice, avocado makes
a rich, very good-looking dressing for cold fish or shellfish.
Garnish with fresh tarragon and finely chopped chives.

Bagel

A firm, hard-crusted white bun, traditionally served with lox.

Bagna Cauda   HC

A hot anchovy sauce that provides a delectable dip for **crudités** but should be avoided by slimmers. It is usually served over a flame to keep it warm while you dunk your raw vegetables. *Blend together 8 fl oz (just under ¼ litre) of heated olive oil, 4 oz (100 g) of mashed anchovy fillets, 4 finely chopped garlic cloves and a dash of tabasco. Transfer everything into a small fondue pot and place it over a burner until it is hot but not boiling. For a more exotic (and even more calorific) Bagna Cauda, add 1 oz (25 g) of crushed walnuts and 2 tablespoons of single cream.* Do include pieces of raw fennel and chunks of red pepper among your crudités for a really fresh tangy flavour. In Italian, Bagna Cauda means, quite literally, a 'hot bath'.

Bain-marie

A large dish or container half-filled with hot water, which can be used for cooking 'sensitive' dishes such as butter-based sauces or fish terrines, which might overcook or disintegrate if they were cooked in or on direct heat.

Baking

A method of cooking fish with dry heat that can be used for almost any fish – fillets, steaks or whole stuffed fish. As fish tends to dry out much more rapidly than meat, it will need some form of added moisture if it is to be baked in an open dish. This could either be butter or oil, brushed on to both the bottom of the baking pan before the fish is placed in it, and then on top of the fish before it goes in the oven, or a little wine or fish stock poured over the fish before cooking and then used for basting during the cooking process. Salt and pepper should be added to the fish before pouring in the wine or stock. A few chopped fresh or dried herbs will make a truly discernible difference.

Oily fish, like herrings, sardines and mackerel, generally need no extra oil – they can be brushed with lemon juice, and basted with that during the cooking process. Or score the surface several times with a sharp knife and rub a little grainy mustard mixed with lemon juice and black pepper into each small slit.

Lean fish, such as cod or plaice, are better baked en papillote, in an envelope of either aluminium **foil** or greaseproof paper. Fish should be placed on foil on top of a bed of finely chopped vegetables or fresh herbs or both, and moistened slightly with a little wine or fish stock, or a tiny dab of butter. Slimmers should stick to fresh herbs and lemon juice.

When baking fish in an open dish, the oven should be pre-heated to 400 °F/200 °C/Gas Mark 6, and a cooking time of 10 minutes per inch of thickness allowed (measure the centre of the fish or the fillet). Baking in foil will require another 5 minutes per inch. If you are baking frozen fish, double the time and add another 5 minutes if the frozen fish is to be cooked in foil.

Barbel   100 barbeau/oily, round

This fresh-water fish found in swift-flowing streams has very tasty white flesh, but it is extremely bony. Treat as **carp**.

Barbequing

Most fish can be barbequed or charcoal-grilled, but oily fish like sardines, herrings and mackerel are best suited to barbequing, as are the thicker cuts of fish, like chunky swordfish, tuna or shark steaks. Whole round fish and steaks can be placed directly on the grill, which should be oiled first to prevent sticking. Thinner flat fish or fillets of fish should either be wrapped in foil or placed on top of a sheet of foil on the grill. If you pierce the foil with a fork in several places, the aroma of the charcoal will get through to the fish. Long-handled double-sided hinged wire racks are also useful for barbequing flat fish or thinner cuts.

Barbequing does tend to dry fish out, so all fish, even oily, should be basted often during barbequing. Lean fish will keep their moisture if they are **marinated** prior to cooking, then basted throughout with the marinade mixture – usually a combination of oil, herbs and lemon juice or wine. Tails and gills should be removed from the whole fish but leave the skin on – even on fillets – to prevent drying out.

Skewers are another great barbeque aid. Cut any firm textured fish into bite-sized chunks, marinate for an hour, thread on to a skewer and place on an oiled grill, basting with the marinade while you cook. If you alternate your fish chunks with whole prawns it will look, and taste, even more interesting. During the cooking process sprinkle herbs – especially rosemary or fennel – on to the coals for a wonderful aroma.

Given that all barbeques give out differing amounts of heat, it is difficult to set a cooking time. The best method is simply to keep testing the fish until it comes away from the bone.

Barracuda   O   170 brochet de mer/round

A large, tuna-type of fighting fish found in the South Atlantic, though smaller barracuda are now being flown into the UK from the Gulf of Oman. There is a rumour that seems to emanate from somewhere in the Caribbean that very large barracuda can be poisonous, this has never been confirmed. Little ones – under two feet – are usually filleted and treated like **tuna** or **shark**; even smaller fish can be fried.

Basil

To many people the most magical of all the herbs. It is not surprising to discover that basil was once decreed a royal plant: only the sovereign was allowed to harvest it – and then only with golden shears. Add fresh basil to a home-made tomato sauce and you can turn a simple cod kebab into a royal treat. Try adding fresh basil to mussels and pasta with fresh tomato **sauce**. In the south of France they stuff red mullet with chopped fresh basil leaves, brush the fish with a little olive oil then grill or bake them en papillote with a sprig of basil inside the envelope, and top them with a slice of basil **butter**. Basil butter made with purple basil (softer, fuller-flavoured than green basil) and chives tastes magnificent on a simple baked sea bream, and a tomato and basil butter transforms simple grilled or sautéed prawns. Fresh basil can also be used to make a mouthwatering potato and basil purée to serve beneath chilled **prawns**. But probably the best-known basil sauce is pesto, a little of which (for it is very rich) is a wonderful accompaniment to plain grilled fresh red mullet: *Chop 2 generous fistfuls of fresh basil leaves and place them in a blender with 1 chopped garlic clove and 1 oz (25 g) of pine nuts. Blend, then slowly dribble in ¼ pint (1.5 dl) olive oil, as though making mayonnaise. When mixed, add 4 tablespoons grated pecorino cheese and 4 tablespoons parmesan cheese. Blend till mixed, adding salt if necessary.* Pesto freezes well, so make plenty in summer when basil is in season.

Bass   L   102 bar or loup de mer/round

A quite delicious sea fish that can occasionally be found in fresh water estuaries from Spring through to Autumn. Much prized by Chinese restaurants who often treat it with greater respect than their occidental peers. Because of the demand, it is somewhat over-priced in this country, making it an expensive, though worthwhile, treat.

There are two types of bass: the striped bass (bar) from the Atlantic and the common sea bass from the Mediterranean (called the loup de mer because it wolfs down everything in sight). In France, especially in southern France, there is sometimes confusion over which bass you are being offered. When bar is included on the menu it very often means loup de mer, which is less delicate than its Atlantic cousin. But both are quite delicious.

Small sea bass can be steamed (as in most Chinese restaurants) or charcoal-grilled. During the summer they are
magnificent barbequed – tastier charcoal-grilled – especially
over dried rosemary or fennel twigs, and served with a full-
flavoured savoury **butter** such as anchovy. Large bass lend

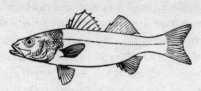

Sea-bass

themselves to **stuffing** (try breadcrumbs well-laced with
garlic and fresh herbs) and **braising** with wine and just a
little good olive oil. For a special occasion try fillets of sea
bass en croûte – topped with a crust of herbs and brioche
crumbs: *Brush 4 large fillets of sea bass with clarified butter
and a squeeze of lemon juice, place on a baking tray and
grill for 2–3 minutes on each side, depending on the
thickness (see* **Canadian Theory**), *basting lightly with butter
and lemon juice. Set them aside in a warm place for 10
minutes while preparing the herb crust from 5 oz (125 g) of
very finely chopped brioche crumbs, 3 oz (75 g) of very dry,
finely chopped mixed Provençal herbs, 1 tablespoon of very
finely chopped parsley, salt and pepper mixed together
completely. Place a tablespoon of this brioche mixture on
top of each fillet and pat down gently so that each fillet is
completely covered. Place a small pool of* **Beurre Blanc** *on
each warmed plate. Flash the fillets quickly under a very hot
grill for a few seconds until the brioche topping is golden,
then carefully position each fillet in the centre of the beurre
blanc pool and serve immediately.*

When very fresh, sea bass is delicious **marinated**. Especially in a ceviche with scallops: *Slice 8 fresh, cleaned scallops*

*in half, and lay them in a shallow dish with 8 oz (200 g)
sliced sea bass fillets. Mix together 1 finely chopped chillie,
1 finely chopped garlic clove, ½ oz (12 g) crushed coriander
seeds, ½ oz (12 g) black pepper, 2 crumbled dried bay leaves,
a pinch of chopped chives, the zest of 1 lemon and 1 lime,
the juice of 1 lemon and 3 limes, and 2 tablespoons olive oil.
Pour over the fish and refrigerate for 24 hours. Serve with
sour cream and fresh dill.*

Basting

Basting is pouring the liquid (the wine, stock, or pan juices)
over fish while it is cooking. This is important when baking
in an open dish or barbequing, as fish tends to dry out more
rapidly than meat or poultry, because it has far less fat.

Batter

Fish is better without batter: better for your waistline, better
for your heart, and better for your taste-buds. A 4 oz (100 g)
piece of cod is 85 calories plain grilled or baked. Add batter
to that 4 oz (100 g) of cod, fry it gently (and we're not even
talking about deep-frying) and that piece of cod shoots up
to 225 calories. However, for those who must have their
batter, here is a recipe made with good olive oil (olive oil is
a mono-unsaturate and, as such, is now considered better
for your health than butter which is a saturate): *Mix together
4 oz (100 g) of flour, 2 dessertspoons of olive oil, a pinch of
salt, and 8 tablespoons of warm water. Let this sit for an
hour and just before using add 2 stiffly beaten egg whites.* If
you have some flat beer to hand, try replacing the water
with the same quantity of beer – it lightens the batter, and
adds an interesting flavour but will also add to the calorie
count – 8 tablespoons is about 40–50 calories depending on

the strength of the beer. Mild ale is around 40, a lager, such as Carling – 50.

Bay

A pale green dried leaf (or bright green if you have it in the garden) that is a traditional component of the **bouquet garni** of herbs that is usually included in a **court-bouillon**.

Bearding

The beard on a mussel is the bunch of dried 'threads' which protrude from between the two shells – it's the mussel's apparatus for clinging to the rocks. Ideally, the beard should be removed before cooking. First, run the mussels under fast-flowing cold water to remove external grit, scrub with a stiff brush, then pull out the beard with either your fingers or a pair of tweezers. If you eat a lot of fish or shellfish, you will find it is worth investing in a pair of tweezers for the kitchen – for bearding and boning.

Beer

Can be used in **batter** for frying fish or shellfish, but re-member, beer is about 100 calories per ½ pint (3 dl). In New Zealand they poach trout in beer: *Melt 1 tablespoon butter in an ovenproof dish, and add 4 trout fillets, seasoned with salt and pepper. Sprinkle over 1 small chopped onion, 1 large chopped celery stalk, and 1 tablespoon of chopped parsley. In a mixing jug, combine ¼ pint (1.5 dl) beer, ¼ pint (1.5 dl) water and a ½ teaspoon sugar, then pour over the fish. Cook in a moderate oven 350 °F/180 °C/Gas Mark 5 for 25 minutes. Remove the fish and keep it warm. Strain the liquid and set it aside.*

Melt 2 tablespoons butter in a small pan, stir in 2 table-spoons flour, and cook till frothy. Stir in ¼ pint (1.5 dl) fish liquid and ¼ pint (1.5 dl) milk, and bring slowly to the boil, stirring well until it thickens. Add ¼ teaspoon dry mustard, a pinch cayenne pepper, and salt and pepper to taste, then stir in 4 tablespoons grated cheese. Place a generous pool of sauce on each plate with a trout fillet in the centre and garnish well with chopped parsley.

Beignet

Beignets are French **fritters**: pieces of fish or shellfish dipped in **batter** and then fried very briefly in hot fat. Soft herring roes are often done this way – Beignets de Laitance. The roes are poached in white wine for 3 or 4 minutes, dipped in lemon juice, then in batter and then in fat. The roes themselves are fairly low in calories – but not when fried as beignets. *For four servings, you will need a dozen pairs of good quality herring roes, poached in a little white wine (enough to cover) for 3 minutes, dipped in 2–3 table-spoons lemon juice, then dipped into a batter made from 4 oz (100 g) flour, 2 dessertspoons of oil and 8 tablespoons water or beer, into which has been folded 2 stiffly beaten egg whites. Quickly fry the battered roes on all sides in a little oil or oil and butter until they are golden brown.* Not for slimmers but a very tasty supper dish when served with a mustard **sauce**.

Beurre Blanc

A rich butter **sauce**, traditionally served with freshwater fish such as pike, that have been poached in a wine court-bouillon but also served with poached or grilled flat fish such as John Dory or Brill. See **sauces** for instructions.

Beurre Manié

Kneaded mixture of equal quantities of butter and flour broken into little pieces and added to sauces to thicken them quickly. See **sauces**.

Beurre Noir

Traditionally served with skate that has been poached in a vinegar court-bouillon, beurre noir is a simple butter sauce with added capers and parsley. It is actually dark golden brown in colour, rather than black. See **sauces**.

Billingsgate

The London fish market, once situated in the heart of the City of London and now out to the east in the Docklands area, selling fish from all over the UK, Europe and increasingly all over the world. It is open to the trade (generally fishmongers and restaurants) from 5 a.m. to 10 a.m., Tuesday through until Saturday – which is why some restaurants have no fresh fish on Mondays. Billingsgate has an annual open day for the public which is well worth a visit, though don't wear your Sunday best – you will arrive home reeking of fish!

Bisque   HC

A bisque is a thick fish soup made from a purée of shellfish or crustaceans – crab, lobster and prawn being the most common. The shellfish or crustacean is generally cooked (with its shell) in a white wine **court-bouillon** then removed from the stock and set aside while the liquid is thickened. *For a tasty (but rich) prawn bisque: Sauté 1 finely chopped* carrot, 1 finely chopped onion, 1 stick of celery, 1 leek and a bunch of chopped parsley stalks together in 1 tablespoon of butter and 1 tablespoon of oil. Add 1 lb (400 g) of prawns (unshelled) and stir gently for 2 or 3 minutes. Add ½ pint (3 dl) of white wine and simmer for 15 minutes. Remove the prawns and set aside. To the liquid, add 1 sherry glass of sherry, 1 lb (400 g) of peeled, seeded and chopped tomatoes – or substitute a 15 oz (375 g) tin – 2 beaten egg yolks, a little cayenne pepper plus seasoning, and 1 tablespoon of brandy. Meanwhile, shell the prawns, setting the prawn meat aside, then crush the shells finely in a mortar or a blender and add to the liquid. Add the prawn meat. Simmer for a good hour, pass through a sieve and serve, topped with a swirl of cream or yoghurt and a sprinkling of finely chopped chives.

Blackened Fish   LC

Blackened fish is fish charcoal-grilled or barbequed in a spicy topping which turns black as it cooks. Currently fashionable in the US where it is billed as Cajun cooking, it is very effective on steaks of oily fish such as swordfish and shark. Blackened mackerel done on a charcoal grill is quite delicious and is an excellent source of Omega 3, without any added calories. To make the spicy topping: Mix together 1 tablespoon paprika, 1 teaspoon cayenne pepper, ½ teaspoon white pepper, ½ teaspoon black pepper, 1 teaspoon garlic powder, 1 teaspoon onion powder, ½ teaspoon crushed dried oregano, and ½ teaspoon crushed dried thyme. Brush fish steaks with a little olive oil then sprinkle the spicy seasoning mix all over, making sure the fish is coated. Place the fish on a grill rack and cook on both sides till well blackened on outside and cooked through.

Blanch

Blanching involves a brief immersion in boiling water. Some fish, like squid and octopus, can be softened by blanching. Blanching will also reduce the acidity in some vegetables, particularly onions. Some vegetables like tomatoes are much easier to peel if they are blanched in boiling water for 20 seconds.

Blini

A small yeast-based pancake of Russian origin which is sometimes used as a base for **caviar** and **keta**.

Bloater   285 craquelot/smoked, oily

These are first cousins to kippers – herrings that have not been gutted, but soaked in brine and lightly salted prior to smoking. Charles Dickens fancied them as an after-dinner savoury, grilled and served with melted butter. However, given the calorie content, they should be avoided by anyone watching their weight.

Bluefish   110 tassegal/oily, round

A blue-green game fish looking and tasting something like a large mackerel, but slightly less oily. Try it **blackened** – grilled with Cajun-style spices – or in any of the mackerel dishes.

Boiling

Fish should never be boiled – it is much too delicate – unless you are making soup. Poach it instead, in stock, wine or

skimmed milk that has not yet come to the boil. Save the
boiling water for shellfish and crustaceans.

Boning

It is surprising, the number of people who won't eat fish at
all because of the bones. So if you are going to convert your
non-fish-eating friends and family to the joys of fish, you
can either buy boned fillets from your fishmonger or learn
how to bone a whole fish yourself. Boning a whole fish
gives you a handy cavity to fill with your favourite stuffing.

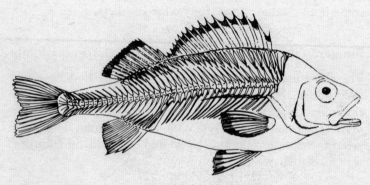

1 Round fish

Round fish are much easier to bone and stuff than flat fish,
which don't give the same sized cavity.

BONING ROUND FISH
You can bone a round fish through the belly or the back
after it has been finned, gilled, gutted, and scaled. If you are
boning through the belly, cut along the belly edge from
behind the head to the start of the tail. Open the fish so that
you can see the backbone and the ribs, which will be covered

with a membrane. In small fish you can usually remove the ribs with your fingers, or with tweezers. With bigger fish you will need a knife to slit the membrane at the end of the rib and slide under each rib toward the backbone. Break each rib off at the backbone. Make a small slit right along each side of the backbone from head to tail. With a knife or scissors cut the backbone at both ends. Salt your fingers to get a good grip, take one end of the backbone and pull it free from the fish. Feel around to make sure there are no small bones left.

To bone a round fish through the back (this works well

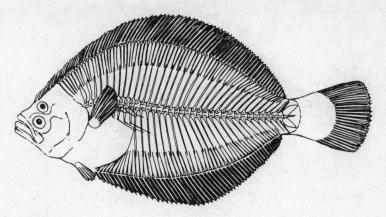

2 Flat fish

with small fish, such as trout that are to be stuffed), place the fish belly down and cut along each side of the backbone from head to tail – not too deeply or you may pierce the belly. Snip the backbone at both ends and, having salted your fingers to get a good grip, grasp the backbone and work it out. Gut, rinse in cold water and feel carefully for any other bones.

BONING FLAT FISH

After gilling and scaling, place fish 'eyeless' side down and slit along the centre of the fish following the backbone from head to tail. Starting at the head, slide the knife between the backbone and the meat and gradually lever the rib bones away from the flesh. Do this on both sides then snip first through the backbone at both ends of the fish then around the outside of the fish where the rib bones join the fins. Salt your fingers and ease the backbone and ribs out – it may help to cut the backbone in the middle as well. Gut the fish, rinse well and check for any other bones.

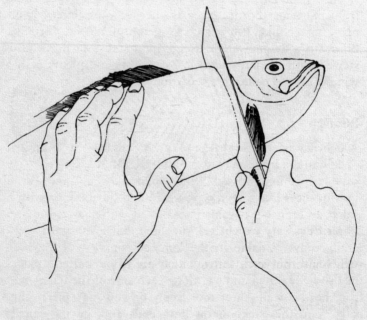

Heading:

Using a heavy knife, slice through the head just behind the gill covers and apply pressure to cut through the backbone.

Bonito $\boxed{O}$ 160 pélamide/oily

A cousin to both the mackerel and the tuna, the bonito is
found occasionally in the UK, but more often in northern
Spain and the Basque country, where its rich, dark meat is
matched with spicy, full-flavoured sauces. Treat like **tuna**
and **marinate** in oil, lemon juice and herbs for a couple of
hours before casseroling in wine, garlic, tomato and herbs.

Bordelaise

A term generally applied to fish cooked in a sauce made
from red wine (Bordeaux being the home of claret). Lamprey, an eel-like fish which is plentiful in the Gironde,
Bordeaux's main river, is usually prepared à la Bordelaise:
stewed with onions, garlic, leeks, carrots and plenty of red
wine. Also the name of a red wine **sauce**.

Botargo

A delicacy made from the roe of grey mullet – also known
as Poutargue in France, and Bottarga in Italy. The roes are
salted, dried and pressed into a cylindrical shape and served
in thin slices like salami with bread and olive oil, or with a
salad. In France it is sometimes served with sour cream and
blinis. It is very expensive (but quite delicious) and is generally only available in the kind of superior delicatessen
which also purveys a range of caviar.

Bouillabaisse

A Bouillabaisse is a soup made from fish, shellfish and
crustacea. The best Bouillabaisse is traditionally prepared in
Marseilles, and even the most ardent Anglophile would have

to admit that a Bouillabaisse cooked in Cornwall will never taste the same as one cooked in Marseilles. You need the Mediterranean blue-mouth (rascasse) and gurnard (grondin) to give Bouillabaisse the right gelatinous quality; anything else is merely soupe de poissons. So, provided you accept that what you are making is probably closer to soupe de poissons than la vraie Bouillabaisse, here is a Bouillabaisse recipe based on that of the late great Marseilles chef, Caillat: *Caillat claimed you would need 5 or 6 different fish, plus shellfish and crustacea. Ideally, gurnard, whiting, conger eel, red mullet and john dory would be among the selection, plus prawns and shellfish. Having gathered together the fish and shellfish (allow 4 lbs (1.6 kilos) of fish and 2 lbs (800 g) of shellfish for 6 people), chop 2 onions, 2 leeks, 4 skinned tomatoes, 4 large garlic cloves, 1 desertspoon of chopped parsley and put them all in a large saucepan with a pinch of dried fennel, a good pinch of saffron and a bay leaf. Add the firm-fleshed fishes (the conger, the dory) chopped into pieces, the prawns and langoustines sliced in half lengthwise, 4 tablespoons of olive oil and salt and pepper to taste. If you are watching your weight, use half the olive oil. Cover with water and boil rapidly for 10 minutes. Add the chopped pieces of the thinner fish (the gurnard, red mullet and the whiting) plus the shellfish and boil for a further 5 minutes. Pour off the liquid into a soup tureen containing thick pieces of untoasted bread. Sprinkle with parsley. Arrange fish and shellfish on a separate platter, and serve.*

Bouquet Garni

A selection of herbs tied together to give flavour to a court-bouillon – a fish stock. The bouquet garni traditionally includes a bay leaf, thyme, marjoram and parsley – but you can make substitutes. Remove the bouquet garni after the fish has been poached and before you use the stock for a sauce or soup.

Bourride

A thick fish soup, rather like a Bouillabaisse without the prawns and shellfish, but with the addition of wine, orange peel and **Aïoli**. *Cover the chopped fish (several different varieties, such as monkfish, turbot or squid) with 2 large chopped onions, 1 chopped leek, 2 chopped tomatoes and 4 cloves of garlic, saffron, the peel of ½ small orange, and a bouquet garni with a ½ pint (3 dl) each of white wine and water, plus 1 tablespoon of olive oil, and boil for 15 minutes. Remove fish to a separate platter, as with Bouillabaisse, and strain the remaining liquid through a sieve. Mix 1 egg yolk with 1 cup of Aïoli and blend this carefully into the liquid. Heat without boiling and serve, like Bouillabaisse, over bread in a soup tureen.*

Braising

Braising is a cooking method using an airtight container and just a little liquid – almost a combination of covered baking and steaming. It is an ideal method for cooking whole fish, provided your covered pan is large enough (though you can use well-fitted foil to cover a baking tin). Place the whole fish on a bed of finely diced vegetables (firm ones like onions and carrots may need to be softened in a small pan first – either in a little butter, a little fish stock or in a little wine; the microwave is good for this). Sprinkle the fish with fresh herbs or add a bouquet garni, season well with salt, pepper and lemon juice or lime, then moisten the fish and the vegetables with either fish **fumet** (concentrated stock) or wine. The liquid should come less than half way up the fish. Cover tightly and cook in a moderate oven using the **Canadian Theory** of timing – 10 minutes per inch plus an extra 5 minutes for each inch if the dish is covered. Baste with the juices several times during cooking.

Brandade $\boxed{\text{HC}}$

A term used most often to describe a purée of salt cod, garlic, oil, and milk or cream, that has the consistency of mashed potatoes. Weight watchers should read no further. Others should: *Soak 1 lb (400 g) of salt cod over night, poach it for 10 minutes in water, then drain and flake the flesh into a saucepan with 2 tablespoons of hot olive oil and a clove of crushed garlic. Beat it to a paste with a wooden spoon – or pop it into the blender. Then, with the heat very low, slowly add, drop by drop, ½ pint (3 dl) of olive oil, beating all the time. Then, also very slowly, add ¼ pint (1.5 dl) of boiled milk (or, if you're feeling wicked, ¼ pint (1.5 dl) single cream), stirring constantly, until it has the thickness of creamy mashed potatoes. Serve Brandade in a large bowl with triangles of toast.*

Brandy   50

Can be used to add flavour and zest to some fish dishes, especially shellfish dishes, and shellfish soups. Ignore any recipe book which suggests cognac and keep to the cooking brandy. Save the cognac for the cook.

Bream $\boxed{\text{L}}$ 115 daurade/round

The sea bream (as opposed to the freshwater bream) comes in a number of different colours: black, red and gold – called gilt. As would be expected, the gold is the most highly prized, but all three are tasty fish and somewhat underrated in the UK; they are still a comparatively good buy here. The French value their daurade much more highly and will serve it with the minimum of elaboration to emphasize its flavour – either plain-grilled with a savoury butter, or rubbed with olive oil and baked with fresh herbs. *In the Middle East, they fill a cleaned and scaled 2½ lb (1 kilo) bream with a* **stuffing** *made from: 8 tablespoons cooked rice, 4 tablespoons chopped fresh parsley, 4 tablespoons finely chopped shallots, 1 tablespoon chopped fresh mint, 1 tablespoon pine nuts, 1 small finely chopped tomato, mixed together with 1 table-spoon lemon juice, 1 tablespoon olive oil, ½ teaspoon cumin, a lightly beaten egg and salt and pepper. Stuff the bream, brush the outside lightly with oil and either wrap with foil or bake it in a covered dish at 400°F/200°C/Gas Mark 6, according to the* **Canadian Theory.**

Sea Bream

In the Far East, there is a very simple bream recipe using spring onions, ginger and sesame oil and very small cleaned and scaled bream (one per person): *Slash the skin right through to the bone at 1 inch intervals. Press fine strips of shallots mixed with very fine strips of fresh ginger into these cuts. Brush bream with the juice of 2 lemons mixed with 2 teaspoons of sesame oil. Place on lightly oiled foil, wrap and bake according to the* **Canadian Theory.**

The freshwater bream is found in lakes and rivers throughout the UK, and like most freshwater fish can taste a little muddy if not washed carefully. A good fish for stuffing (something simple like mushrooms, shallots and breadcrumbs) and baking in wine. It can be used in any **carp** recipe, and is ideal for freshwater fish stews or **Matelotes**.

Brill

⌐L⌐ 100 barbue/flat

If you can't afford turbot, settle for its first cousin, the brill. A speckled, yellowy-brown flat fish of a very similar shape to the turbot, the brill has a light, delicate texture which is only now being recognized in the UK for its excellent quality – in France the barbue has long been prized as a gastronomic treat.

Small brill can be slit in half lengthwise, large ones should be cut from head to tail down the middle and cut in transverse slices or **filleted** as a sole.

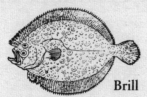

Brill

Brill can be used in any **turbot** recipe, but because of its delicacy, it is particularly well-suited to steaming, poaching, and to cooking en papillote with julienned vegetables and a little fresh ginger: *Soften thinly sliced vegetables (a julienne of carrots, celery and courgettes will give an interesting contrast of colours) by sweating them over a low heat in a little butter or a little fish stock. Place a bed of the vegetables beneath a brill fillet in a covered shallow dish or on a piece of foil. Sprinkle with fresh grated ginger root (about a ¼ teaspoon per fillet), a dash of lime juice and 1 tablespoon of white wine or fish* **fumet** *to moisten each fillet. Close foil or cover dish and cook as per* **Canadian Theory**.

Brine

A solution of salt, water, saltpetre, and sometimes a little sugar with various herbs and spices added to make a preservative for fish. If you are watching your weight buy all canned fish in brine, rather than oil.

Brisling   O 230 round

Young **sprats**, usually canned.

Brochette

The French term for a kebab, or skewer. This is an ideal way of grilling or barbequing fish and shellfish, especially if the chunks of fish are interspersed with colourful slices of vegetable, such as red and green peppers, cucumbers, tomatoes and mushrooms. If barbequing, it helps to **marinate** fish before threading it on to skewers. If grilling, brush fish very lightly with oil before placing under the grill, unless you are using an oily fish such as herring or mackerel. Brochettes can also be **blackened**, with spices sprinkled on to each bite-sized chunk.

Broiling

The American term for grilling in an oven, under direct heat, as opposed to charcoal-grilling which is done over heat.

Buckling   O 234 hareng fumé/round

Herrings, usually without their heads, that have been hot-smoked.

Burbot

L   lotte de rivière/round

A type of freshwater cod found in lakes and streams of southern England and much of France. Treat as **pike** unless you
can obtain the liver, which is very highly regarded in France,
where it is poached in white wine to be eaten during Lent.

Butterfish

L   115 fiatole/round

Sometimes known as pomfret, this type of small sea bream
is not generally more than six inches long, and is found in
the North Atlantic and the Pacific. It is most often deep-
fried, but can also be baked like bream: *Rub with olive oil,*
sprinkle with lemon juice and season well with salt and
pepper. Bake on a bed of softened chopped fennel liberally
moistened with white wine, and cook according to the
Canadian Theory.

Butter

Butter and fish go together almost like wine and cheese –
too well. The thing to remember about butter is that a little
goes a long way. A level tablespoon of butter is approximately 105 calories – an awful lot to come out of your daily
allowance if you are on a calorie-controlled diet. However,
1 teaspoon of butter is only $\frac{1}{3}$ of that – 35 calories, and
when melted will be quite sufficient to brush on to a grilled
fish steak or to cover the bottom of a pan in which you are
softening garlic, onions and tomatoes. If you are more con-
scious of your heart and your health than your waistline,
use olive oil where possible. It is slightly higher in calories
than butter but because it is a mono-unsaturated oil, it is
generally regarded – certainly by all the American 'fish'
doctors – as being a healthier companion for fish than

butter. One of the best ways to use butter with fish is to make it into a savoury butter. Mix the herb, spice or flavouring of your choice with softened butter and seasoning (you can use a blender). Roll the mixture into a long thin cylinder – about the diameter of a ten-pence-piece. Wrap it in foil and freeze it until you need it. Then simply unwrap and slice off as many circles as you require to place on top of your grilled or baked fish. You can pop the savoury butter inside fish for extra flavour, as well as outside before grilling or baking.

You can use your imagination (and whatever herbs you have to hand) when it comes to making savoury butters, but here are some suggestions: *To a basic quantity of 4 oz (100 g) of butter, 1 teaspoon of lemon juice, salt and pepper, add any of the following ingredients:*

Almond: *add 2oz (50 g) blanched almonds.*
Anchovy: *add 1–2 anchovy fillets, well mashed.*
Basil and chive: *add 1 oz (25 g) chopped fresh basil and 1 oz (25 g) chopped chives.*
Basil and tomato: *sauté 2 chopped, peeled and seeded tomatoes together with 1 small chopped clove of garlic. Reduce to a thick consistency – about 2 tablespoons. Cool, then add 1 tablespoon chopped basil and mix with softened butter.*
Coriander: *add 2 oz (50 g) freshly chopped coriander leaves – not seeds.*
Chive: *add 2 oz (50 g) chopped chives.*
Dill: *add 2 oz (50 g) chopped fresh dill.*
Fennel: *gently cook 2 oz (50 g) chopped raw fennel in a little butter. Cool and add to softened butter.*
Ginger/lime: *add 1 teaspoon chopped ginger to the juice and zest of 1 lime.*
Herb: *add a 2 oz (50 g) mixture of fresh green herbs,*

chopped. Try a mixture of chervil, tarragon, dill, even a little parsley.

Lemon/lime: *add the juice and zest of 1 lemon or lime and 1 teaspoon of chopped chives.*

Mustard: *add 1 tablespoon grainy mustard.*

Olive: *add 2 oz (50 g) finely chopped olives, and blend well.*

Orange: *add the juice and zest of 1 small orange and 1 teaspoon chopped chives or parsley.*

Pernod: *add 1 tablespoon Pernod and 1 teaspoon of chopped fresh fennel leaf.*

Red Pepper: *gently cook 2 oz (50 g) chopped red peppers with 1 teaspoon chopped shallot together in a little butter. Cool and blend with softened butter.*

Red Wine: *gently heat 2 tablespoons red wine together with 1 teaspoon chopped chives, and 1 teaspoon chopped shallots. Bring to the boil, then reduce the mixture by half and cool before blending into softened butter.*

Shrimp: *4 oz (100 g) shrimps, pounded.*

Smoked salmon: *4 oz (100 g) smoked salmon, finely chopped.*

Tarragon: *add 2 oz (50 g) fresh tarragon, finely chopped.*

Buying Fish

The Sea Fish Authority is so right when they say make a friend of your fishmonger. There are some wonderful fellows in the retail fish trade (behind the supermarket fish counters as well as in the fish shops) who can be a tremendous help to the novice fish purchaser, and who would be unlikely ever to foist a less than fresh fish off on you. But there are also one or two chaps (fortunately these are few and far between) who would rather see those fish fillets sold (even at a reduced profit) and going to a good home than having to throw them in the bin at the end of the day – even if they

are a day or two past their prime. You hear so many shop-
pers asking anxiously, 'Is it fresh?' When did you last hear a
fishmonger reply, 'Well, actually, no madam, I've been sitting on that little bit of cod for three or four days now,
haven't been able to move it'?

Fish that is not quite fresh is unlikely to do you any harm
(though the same doesn't apply to shellfish). It just won't
taste anywhere near as good as fresh fish. The best way to
tell if a fish is fresh is to look it in the eye – the eye should
be bulging and bright, with black pupils. If it is sunken and
dull with cloudy grey pupils, then the fish is probably not
the catch of the day. The skin should also be in good condition – shiny to look at and springy to the touch. If you
press it, the skin should bounce back without leaving an
indentation. The gills should be red; as a fish starts to age it
goes a brownish-green about the gills. It should also smell,
quite pleasantly, of the sea. Only skate should give out any
tinge of ammonia.

Fish fillets should be firm, moist and shiny; if they are
dull, soft or dry, leave them. There should be no browning
or discolouration at the edges. Fish steaks should also be
firm and tight to the bone. Check that the flesh bounces
back without any indentations. When buying shellfish, check
that the shells are all tightly closed and there is no discolouration at the joints. They should smell just like seaweed
– nothing stronger.

If you are buying a whole fish, count on losing a third to
a half of it when you remove the head, tail and bones. The
bigger the head, the less fish you will be left with. When
buying fish steaks, work on 2 to the pound; fillets, 3 to the
pound, unless you are all on diets then you might get 4
small ones.

Calvados

French apple brandy that will perk up a number of fish dishes, especially good in **Matelote** Normande, a fish soup that is full of mussels.

Canadian Theory

No doubt in response to consumer complaints that fish was difficult to cook, because you never knew when it was done, the Canadian Department of Fisheries spent a great deal of time and effort trying to find out how long the average fish needed cooking – regardless of whether it was being poached, steamed, grilled or baked. It has come up with a rule of thumb, generally referred to as the Canadian Theory, which seems to work every time – for whole fish, for steaks, and for fillets.

Simply measure your fish at the thickest part and for every inch of thickness cook it for 10 minutes. If you are cooking in foil, add 5 minutes on for every inch, and if you are cooking frozen fish, double the time. If you are baking a stuffed fish, measure the thickness after it is stuffed. The oven should be at 420 °F–450 °F/220 °C–250 °C/Gas Mark 7. For example: if you are grilling a fillet that is only ½ inch thick, then the total cooking time should be 5 minutes – 2½ minutes on each side.

Once fish is done it should be opaque and almost flaky when prodded with a skewer at the thickest part. If in any doubt, *undercook* your fish. Most people prefer to err on the 'safe' side and overcook it. The reason many people believe that fish is boring is that they've only ever eaten fish that has had all the flavour cooked out of it.

Caper

The bud of the caper bush which is pickled in vinegar. Used as a seasoning, it is most often found in fish cookery sprinkled over skate in a **beurre noir**, in a Sauce **Gribiche**, or a Sauce **Tartare**, both good with shellfish.

Carp   O   150 carpe/oily

A toothless freshwater fish with gold-green scales, the carp can grow to an enormous age and size – over 100 lbs (45 kilos) in weight, and up to 150 years old. Unlike most freshwater fish, it is widely available in the better fish-mongers from the commercial carp farms in Holland and France. Like the freshwater bream carp needs very careful cleaning (at least 2 good soaks in salted water followed by 1 soak in water with a little vinegar added) to rid it of the muddy taste of a slow-moving stream. Some of the land-locked Eastern European countries with no ready access to sea fish are enthusiastic carp eaters (it is also farmed in many Eastern bloc countries) and have a variety of colourful carp recipes, many involving fruit and nut stuffings. Dried apricots, raisins, almonds and chestnuts are often featured.

Perhaps the most famous chestnut stuffing for carp was found at Alice's, the restaurant immortalized in song: *Clean, wash and dry a 3 lb (1.2 kilos) carp, and season well both inside and out. Soften a large chopped onion in 2 tablespoons of butter, then add 2 slices of bread that have been soaked in a little white wine and squeezed dry, 1 tablespoon chopped parsley, 2 finely chopped spring onions, 1 minced garlic clove, 1 teaspoon salt, ¼ teaspoon each black pepper, mace, thyme, crushed bay leaf and 12 chestnuts, boiled and peeled (tinned will do). Mix well, cool then bind with a beaten egg. Stuff the fish with this mixture, securing it well with thread or skewers and set aside for 2 hours. Place the stuffed fish in a large deep dish, cover with 2 cups of white wine and bake at 375 °F/190 °C/Gas Mark 5 for about 20 minutes, basting half-way through. Remove from the oven, baste, and sprinkle liberally with cracker crumbs (or dried breadcrumbs). Drizzle over 2 tablespoons melted butter, and bake for a further 20 minutes.*

The Hungarians have a carp soup which, like many Hungarian dishes, is generously spiced with paprika: *Make a fish stock by adding 1 lb (400 g) of carp trimmings, including the well-cleaned head and bones, 1 each sliced red and green pepper, 1 large chopped garlic clove, 2 large sliced onions, 2 large ripe tomatoes, peeled, seeded and chopped, and 6 green peppercorns to 2 pints (1.1 litres) water. Simmer for half an hour, then strain the stock, retaining only the broth. Add to this broth: 1 generous tablespoon of paprika, 2 tablespoons of finely chopped parsley, 1 tablespoon of lemon juice and a few drops of tabasco. Return to the heat and stir well. Add 1 lb (400 g) of carp cut into cubes and simmer for 10 minutes. Serve sprinkled with fresh chopped parsley.*

Carpaccio

Carpaccio used to be a term reserved for paper-thin sliced raw beef dressed with very good olive oil, in the best Italian restaurants. Now it also applies to very thinly sliced raw fish – Carpaccio of salmon or of tuna now appears on some extremely smart menus. In New York, a tuna Carpaccio arrives dressed with lime juice, freshly chopped coriander and purest virgin olive oil. The oil and the lime juice are mixed together with the fresh coriander then dribbled over finely sliced raw tuna and left to marinate for half an hour before serving. An even more stunning combination is the tuna Carpaccio alternated with wafer-thin slices of fresh raw salmon – an attractive contrast of colours and textures. Fish must be very, very fresh to survive as Carpaccio. For those whose noses turn up at the very mention of raw anything, marinated raw fish tastes much better than it sounds; the acid in the lemon or lime reacts with the fish to turn it opaque and 'cook' it. *Slice 1 lb (400 g) very fresh tuna (or very fresh salmon) very thinly and place on 4 individual platters. Make sure that the slices are not overlapping. Mix together 3 tablespoons fresh lime juice, 4 tablespoons very good olive oil, 6 tablespoons chopped fresh coriander leaves, and ½ a small, very finely chopped, fresh green chillie pepper. Spoon the dressing over the fish, and garnish with lime slices. Wrap each plate in foil and chill in refrigerator for at least 30 minutes.*

Casserole

In French cuisine, a casserole was originally a dish that was made with a rice base. In a broader sense it has come to denote a dish that is made in a single ovenproof container that combines meat or fish with either rice, pasta or potatoes

– a meal in a single pot, like a **Cotriade**. Not to be confused with Cassoulet, which is a rich stew from the south-west of France, usually incorporating haricot beans, preserved goose or duck and sausages.

Catfish   L 178 loup marin/round

In the UK, the name catfish was most often applied to the pinky-coloured rock salmon or **dogfish**. These days it refers either to the wolf-fish or to the freshwater catfish, which is imported live from Belgium, where it is farmed; a strange, feline-looking fellow with long wriggling whiskers – just like a cat. It mainly appeared only in oriental cuisine but is beginning to enjoy a wider audience as the vogue for **Creole** cooking spreads. Care should be taken when cleaning – the spines are fairly sharp. Small catfish can be skinned, dipped in egg and breadcrumbs and shallow-fried; larger ones taste good cut into bite-sized pieces and stewed slowly in a spicy Creole-style sauce of red and green peppers, garlic, chillie peppers, and a generous dash of cayenne.

Caviar   O   ♡ 330 caviare/oily, roe

The good news is that caviar prices are coming down. The least expensive of the caviars, Sevruga, is now retailing at around £12.00 an ounce. The reason for the falling prices is mainly increased competition, as caviar merchants woo a whole new market of caviar-lovers created by cruise-ship passengers and first-class fliers discovering these exquisite little sturgeon eggs for the first time.

  In the last century, caviar used to be produced in France, the US and even the UK. But pollution has killed off most of the world's sturgeon stocks and now ninety-five per cent of the world's caviar comes from Russia and Iran, with the remainder coming from China, France and a little from Italy.

There are three major commercial caviars, each named after the sturgeon it comes from: Beluga is the largest of the fish – sometimes weighing up to 2,000 lbs (900 kilos) – and its roe, which are black or grey in colour, are the largest and most expensive; Osietra or Oestrova is next down in size and cost, and has smaller goldish-tinged grains. Third, and most plentiful, is Sevruga, which is smaller than Beluga but also grey-black in colour. A comparative newcomer to the European caviar market is the Chinese Keluga, which also has a golden tinge to its grains. Also available in some UK caviar outlets is the old Russian favourite, Pressed Caviar, a combination of 'overripe' Beluga and Oscietra grains pressed together to look rather like lumpy black jam with a wonderfully concentrated caviar flavour. If a caviar jar bears the word Malasol, it simply means lightly salted.

Many restaurants serve caviar with chopped onions, chopped eggs and even capers. Good caviar has such a perfectly exquisite taste that it needs no accompaniment – except for blinis or a slice of crisp warm wholewheat toast, and a glass of champagne or a tiny iced glass of very cold vodka. But unless you are exceedingly rich and can afford to buy Royal Beluga (the king of the caviars) from Harrods in their 4 lb (1.8 kilo) tins (a bargain at £1,347.00), don't waste your caviar on making sauces – use Danish **lumpfish** roe.

The Russians have long believed caviar to be a powerful aphrodisiac, which is perhaps why they lead the world in caviar consumption. It is almost as expensive, comparatively, in the USSR as it is in the West. It certainly is high in essential minerals and in Omega 3.

Cephalopod

The collective name for molluscs such as squid, octopus, cuttlefish and suppion. So called by the Greeks because they have no body – only a head (kephale) and feet (podos).

Ceviche

Also spelt Seviche in some parts of the world. This is a cold marinated raw fish dish that makes an unusual starter. It can be made with any firm white fish – even cod – or some shellfish, particularly scallops. It is very popular in Central and South America and the following recipe is the Mexican version: *As a starter for 6 you will need: 1 lb (400 g) of red snapper fillets (or any firm white fish), 1 lb (400 g) of roughly chopped ripe tomatoes, 2 small finely chopped onions, 1 chopped green chillie, 8 tablespoons tomato juice, 4 table-spoons tomato sauce, 10 chopped green olives, 1 tablespoon chopped coriander, 1 teaspoon oregano, 1 tablespoon of olive oil, a clove of garlic, finely chopped, 4 tablespoons lemon juice, ¼ lb (100 g) of fresh green peas and salt and black pepper. Cut the fish into small cubes and marinate in lemon juice and salt for 30 minutes. Mix all other ingredients together. Drain and wash the fish, then mix into the sauce and serve on lettuce leaves or as a fish cocktail with a sprinkling of coriander leaves.* North of the border in California, Ceviche is sometimes sweetened slightly with the addition of 8 tablespoons orange juice. For an even simpler marinated fish dish see **Kokoda**.

Champagne   22

Champagne is the perfect companion for fish, shellfish and crustaceans: cold poached salmon with champagne, oysters and champagne, lobster and champagne. Better to drink with than to cook with, but champagne left-overs make wonderful sauces and poaching liquids. In Sydney, they poach oysters in champagne then serve them warm on a brilliant green **watercress** purée decorated with darker green coriander leaves. Or use your left-overs to make a marvellously light champagne **vinaigrette** to pour over chilled prawns.

Char   155 omble chevalier/round, oily

A freshwater salmon trout with a flaky orange flesh. Treat as **trout**.

Chervil

A pretty green herb with a leaf that is a cross between coriander and parsley. It teams up well with tarragon and is an important (though not essential) ingredient of a good **green sauce**. With coriander, it makes an interesting accompaniment to a warm scallop salad.

Chillie

A small, very hot pepper. The green ones are used to add spice to Mexican, Latin American and American Creole cooking. Chillie is too strong for most fish dishes, though green chillie is used in the raw fish dish **Ceviche** and red chillie is used to make the very hot **Peri-Peri** sauce which is often served in Africa and Asia as a dip for prawns.

Chive

This long thin green herb has been likened to a spring onion,

without the bite. Chives work well with a wide range of fish
– either as a savoury **butter**, a seasoning for some **stuffings**,
or chopped and scattered as a garnish. A hot chive **sauce**,
made by adding very finely chopped chives to hollandaise
sauce, works surprisingly well with grilled salmon. The
easiest way to chop chives very finely is to line the ends
up and snip off miniscule sections with a pair of small
scissors.

Chowder   HC

Originally a French term for a fish stew (from the name of
the pot, a chaudron), Chowder now denotes a very thick
fish or shellfish soup, especially clams. American Clam
Chowder traditionally includes bacon, potatoes, chicken
stock and milk or cream, as well as the clams. If you are
ordering it in New England, you probably won't need a
second course, it is so filling. New England Clam Chowder
doesn't contain tomatoes; Manhattan Clam Chowder does,
but has no milk or cream. Apparently, the argument over
whether Chowders should contain tomatoes or milk became
so fierce at one time that the State of Maine on the New
England coast introduced a bill into the State Legislature to
make tomatoes in Clam Chowder illegal.

Here is a legal Clam Chowder recipe: *Boil 1 lb potatoes
(400 g), cut into cubes, for 5 minutes, then drain. Place ¼ lb
(100 g) chopped lean bacon in a large heavy-bottomed pot
and cook till crisp. Remove the bacon with a slotted spoon,
and soften 1 finely chopped onion in the bacon fat. Add the
potatoes and stir well. Pour in 1½ pints (just under 1 litre)
fish* **stock** *and simmer for 10–15 minutes till the potatoes
are soft but still cubed. Add 1½ pints (almost 1 litre) clam
meat (tinned if you can't get fresh) and their juice, plus salt
and fresh black pepper, ½ pint (3 dl) of milk (or cream) and*

*heat through gently – do not boil. Sprinkle the chowder
with the bacon and chopped parsley before serving.*

Cider   8

Cider is used frequently in fish dishes from Normandy (the
region having a long coastline and a plentiful supply of
apples). The Normans use cider in their **Matelote**; cod works
well with cider and apples and a hint of **clove**, so do some
smoked fish. Incidentally, iron or aluminium saucepans
should never be used when cooking with cider – the metal
turns the cider black.

Cioppino   HC

California's answer to the East Coast Chowders – this one
includes tomatoes, and lots of them. It is often made with a
firm, white fish, crab, prawns and shellfish, though this
Californian version leaves out the white fish in favour of: *8
prawns, 8 clams on the shell, 12 scallops or mussels (or
both), a 1 lb (400 g) cooked crab and ¼ lb (100 g) cooked
shrimps. Clean and prepare shellfish. Then make a stew base
from 2 large chopped leeks, 1 chopped onion, 1 clove of
garlic, 1 tablespoon parsley, ¼ teaspoon oregano, ¼ teaspoon saffron, 2 bay leaves, ½ tablespoon salt, ½ teaspoon
black pepper, 4 tablespoons olive oil, 1 pint (6 dl) red wine,
2 × 15 oz (375 g) tins diced tomatoes and ¼ pint (1.5 dl)
canned tomato sauce. Put all the vegetables and seasoning
into a large saucepan and simmer for 15 minutes. Add the
wine and simmer uncovered for 1 hour. Add the tomatoes
and simmer for 30 minutes. 5 minutes before serving, add
all the shellfish except the crab and shrimp and simmer. 1
minute before serving add cooked crab and shrimp.*

Clam

A small oval-shelled bi-valve mollusc which is much more popular in the US than it is here, appearing on both coasts in the ubiquitous clam **Chowder**. However, the contents of the average clam Chowder – it usually includes bacon and cream – rather negate the low-calorie benefits of the clam. The French eat them raw (pallourdes on the Atlantic coast, clovisses in Provence), and they are most often found in the UK served up in superior seafood platters to be eaten raw like oysters with lemon juice. Most English clams are grown in the Solent, in beds developed from clams that arrived last century clinging to the hulls of foreign sailing ships.

If you have some very fresh clams, serve them Mexican-style: Remove the meat, marinate it briefly in lemon juice, garlic and freshly chopped coriander then return the meat to the shells to serve as a starter. Clams can also be added to any fish soup requiring shellfish – use tinned for soup if you can't get fresh. Fresh clams should be opened by **shucking** them like oysters, or by popping them into a warm oven for just a few minutes till they start to open. Clam juice is a useful substitute for fish stock, and clams are, of course, extremely popular with **pasta** in vongole sauce.

Tinned baby clams can be turned very simply into an eye-catching mini-soufflé as a starter: *Drain an 8 oz (200 g) tin of baby clams (smoked are better) and marinate very briefly in the juice of ½ lemon mixed with a little chopped parsley. Dry the clams and put them in a bowl with 3 tablespoons mayonnaise (low-cal or half mayonnaise and half yoghurt if you are weight-watching), the zest of ½ lemon, 1 teaspoon lemon juice, ¼ teaspoon paprika, salt and pepper. Set aside in a cool place. With a 2–3 inch circular cookie cutter, cut 12 circles out of bread slices and toast on one side only. Whisk 3 egg whites till stiff and fold them into the clam and mayonnaise mixture. Place a high mound of this mixture on each round of bread, arrange on a baking tray and bake in a hot oven, 425 °F/220 °C/Gas Mark 7 for about 5 minutes, until well-risen and lightly browned. Serve immediately – they should still be creamy in the middle.*

Cleaning

Most fishmongers will clean your fish for you, but if you should catch your own or be presented with a whole fresh

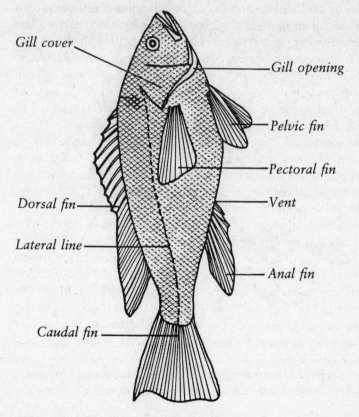

Gill cover

Gill opening

Pelvic fin

Pectoral fin

Dorsal fin

Vent

Lateral line

Anal fin

Caudal fin

fish, you'll need to know how to clean it. First give it a good rinse to wash off any surplus slime, then lay out a sheet of newspaper on the sink top and place the fish on top of it. Salt the fingers of your left hand with plenty of salt to give you a good grip on the fish and grasp it firmly by the tail. With a sharp knife scrape the scales using short, sharp strokes from the tail towards the head. Do the same on the other side, adding more salt to your fingers if necessary. Rinse the fish in cold water.

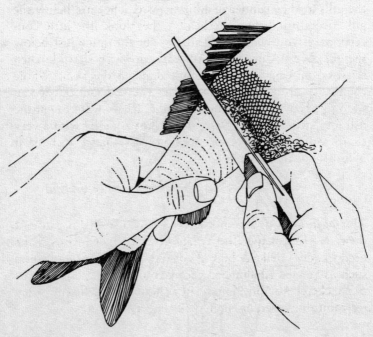

Scaling:

1 Salt fingers and grasp fish firmly by the tail, over a large sheet of newspaper.
2 Scrape the scales with short, sharp strokes, from tail to head.
3 Rinse well in fast-flowing cold water.

To gut the fish, make a slit from below the gill opening behind the head to the base of the tail. Extract the roe (the two long sacs of eggs found in female fish) in case you want to include them in the fish stuffing – you will need to cut them free carefully to avoid breaking them – then pull out all innards (called viscera) with your fingers. You may need to use a teaspoon to scrape off the bits of kidney that are still clinging to the fish. Rinse very well with cold water.

If you are cooking your fish with the head left on, remove the gills as they can leave a bitter taste. They are below the gill covers just below the head – they look like little concertinas. If you want the head off, cut the spine just below the gill covers. Cut the fins off carefully with sharp kitchen scissors, making sure you don't damage the skin. Whole round fish are usually cooked with the skin on, but if you wish to remove it, see under **skinning**. If you want to cut the fish into steaks immediately, slice it horizontally with a very sharp knife, making each steak no less than $\frac{3}{4}$ inch or it will dry out in cooking.

Clove

The dried buds of a tropical evergreen, so called because of their nail-like shape (from *clavus* – a nail). Cloves can be used to add a delicate hint of spice to some soups and stews such as Stewed **Abalone** and to flavour cooking liquids – as in **Mackerel** Au Vin Blanc. They should be used with some restraint, however, as the flavour is very strong.

Cockle   54 coque/shellfish

A round brown mollusc about 1 inch in diameter and usually eaten raw, but which can be cooked, or **pickled** in vinegar. Cockles need to be soaked in salt water for several hours to clean them before cooking, in the same way you would treat a **mussel**. Marinated in lemon juice, they are an interesting

Cockle

addition to a seafood salad. Cockles are high in selenium – good news for a flagging libido – and have a higher iron content than most other fish or shellfish, so if you are at all anaemic, eat cockles.

Coconut

The milk of the coconut is used in Tahiti and Fiji in a delicious marinated fish salad (called Poisson Cru in Tahiti and **Kokoda** in Fiji). You can buy coconut milk at most Indian provision shops or you can make your own by mixing 8 tablespoons finely grated coconut with 8 tablespoons warm skimmed milk and leaving for half an hour before straining.

Cod $\boxed{L}$ 84 cabillaud/round

The poor old cod is so readily available (it's one of the few fish you'll find at the Billingsgate Fish Market fifty-two weeks of the year) and so adaptable that it suffers from a rather poor press, and a resultingly less than chic image. But fresh cod can be quite delicious, even if baked very simply en papillote or in **foil** with wine and plenty of fresh herbs. You can use cod in almost any recipe calling for a large lean fish, though it is not at its best plain grilled, and is not really delicate enough for steaming; it needs stronger treatment and full-flavoured sauces. Try brushing cubes of cod lightly with oil and lemon juice, seasoning generously with salt and pepper, then grilling them on a skewer with slices of red and green pepper, and serving with a tangy fresh **tomato sauce**.

Cod also bakes well: *You can bake either steaks or fillets in the Greek style by softening 1 finely chopped onion, 1 chopped clove of garlic, and 1 green pepper and 1 red pepper, seeded and thinly sliced, together in 2 tablespoons of olive oil. Add a dozen or so stoned and roughly chopped black olives, a 12 oz (300 g) can of drained chopped tomatoes, ½ teaspoon dried oregano, ½ teaspoon crushed coriander seeds, a crumbled bay leaf, 4 tablespoons fish* **stock**, *4 tablespoons white wine (retsina would be perfect), and simmer for 5 minutes. If you have no fish stock, double the amount of wine. Brush the base and sides of an oven-proof dish with olive oil and lay the cod steaks or fillets flat within it. Pour over the sauce then sprinkle with 4 oz (100 g) finely crumbled feta cheese. Bake in a moderate oven 350 °F/180 °C/Gas Mark 4, according to the* **Canadian Theory.** *Garnish with black olives.*

Cod Cheek   O

Like roes, cod cheeks are high in Omega 3. Many fisherfolk consider the cheeks of cod (frequently discarded with the head by those who have never tried them) to be a great delicacy. They are most often served lightly boiled in enough water to cover, with 1 chopped onion and seasoned lightly with salt, pepper and ½ teaspoon vinegar.

Cod, Salted   158 morue/dried

Cod that has been salted and dried for preservation is

available at some specialist food shops in the UK. It looks rather like dried-out chamois leather, and apparently will keep for several years if it has been properly salted. It needs to be soaked in water for at least 24 hours before cooking. The French make a creamy dip of salt cod called **Brandade** de morue with lots of olive oil, garlic and cream – definitely not for dieters. In Provence they poach it, cool it and mix it with olives, tomatoes and basil in a salad. The Portuguese are one of Europe's greatest users of salt cod (they call it Baccalao) and have a wide variety of recipes, including a tasty stew with wine, tomatoes, potatoes and plenty of garlic: *Cut 1½ lbs (600 g) salt cod into pieces, rinse thoroughly under running water, then cover with cold water in a covered container. Leave in the refrigerator overnight. Rinse again, then place the pieces of salt cod in a large pan with 1 bay leaf, ½ teaspoon thyme and 2 sprigs of parsley. Cover, bring to boil, then remove from the heat and leave to stand for 20 minutes.*

Meanwhile: Chop 2 cloves garlic, 2 medium-sized onions and 3 peeled and seeded tomatoes. Place half of this mixture in the base of a well-oiled baking dish, and lay the well-drained fish fillets on top. Spread the other half of the tomato mixture on top of the fish and dribble over 4 tablespoons olive oil. Bake the fish at 375 °F/190 °C/Gas Mark 5 for approximately 30 minutes or until it flakes easily.

Coley $\boxed{\text{L}}$ 85 lieu noir/round

This is known also as saithe and coalfish. The coley is not greatly sought after in the UK because of its rather unattractive grey-coloured flesh. However don't be put off by its unprepossessing appearance – coley flesh turns white during cooking, so it is a perfectly acceptable substitute for cod in a fish soup or stew, fish pie or fishcakes or any casserole-style recipe calling for firm white fish. Treat as **cod**.

Conger Eel   220 congre/round, oily

Found in both the Atlantic and the Mediterranean, the conger eel is a fairly unattractive fish without a great following in this country – though a century ago it was much more popular. Because it is so full-flavoured it makes a welcome addition to rich soups and stews like the Catalan fish stew, **Zarzuela**. *Try adding ½ lb (200 g) conger eel (get the fishmonger to chop it up for you) to your next fish* **pie**. *Poach it for 10 minutes in enough red wine to cover it, remove the skin and bones and add to the fish pie mixture.*

Cooking Time

See **Canadian Theory**.

Coral   ☐ O ☐

The name for the roe sacs in scallops and crustaceans. In scallops they are pale orange; in lobsters a dark greeny-grey, turning pink when cooked. Lobster coral can be used to make coral **butter** by mixing the raw roe with double its weight of softened butter. It will look a strange charcoal shade when raw, but it will turn a pretty coral pink when heated. Like other roes, coral is high in Omega 3.

Coriander

The leaves of fresh coriander are also known as cilantro (one of the signature ingredients of California cuisine) and chinese parsley (which plays an important part in Asian cooking). Its light, fresh, slightly spicy taste can add an intriguing touch to an overly gentle fish or shellfish dish. In Los Angeles grilled scallops take on an exotic air when served up with chervil and coriander vinaigrette. In New York coriander stars in at least half a dozen smart new dishes, including a shrimp **stuffing** for sole; a dressing for raw sea bass mixed with olive oil, lemon juice and basil; and again with basil, parsley and fresh ginger in a stewed **mussel** dish. It is such an attractive leaf that it makes a perfect decoration instead of the more usual chopped chives or chopped parsley. But use it sparingly: it has quite a distinctive taste, which some people find a little overpowering.

Coriander seeds have quite a different flavour – with an aromatic, almost sweet spiciness. They are crushed before use and appear mainly in fish **curries** and in some Greek fish dishes, where they are crushed in the oil used to brush over whole fish or fish kebabs before cooking.

Coquille St Jacques

French name for **scallops**.

Cotriade

Brittany's version of the **Bouillabaisse**, which omits the shellfish but includes potatoes which are cooked with the fish in the broth. Like Bouillabaisse and **Bourride**, the fish (and the potatoes) are served on a separate platter and the soup is poured into a tureen over thick slices of bread: *Soften 2 cloves of garlic and 2 large chopped onions together in a tablespoon of oil, in a large heavy-bottomed saucepan. Add 2 large, roughly chopped potatoes, a bouquet garni, a good pinch of marjoram, 1 heaped tablespoon chopped parsley and 2 pints hot fish* **stock**. *Bring to the boil and simmer for 15 minutes. Add about 2–2½ lbs (about 1 kilo) of various*

*fish fillets (cod, coley, hake, halibut, mackerel), small whole
fish (sardines, smelts) and conger eel cut into chunks. Cook
over a high heat for 10 minutes or until the fish and potatoes
are soft but not mushy. Remove the fish and potatoes with
a slotted spoon and arrange on a platter. Season the liquid
with lemon juice, salt and pepper, then strain into a tureen
over thick slices of fresh bread. Serve this alongside the fish
platter, accompanied by olive oil and vinegar.*

Coulibiac

Also called Kulibiaka, this is a Russian fish dish involving
salmon, rice and herbs, usually in layers, wrapped in a light
brioche-type pastry: *Prepare (or buy) ½ lb (200 g) of flaky
pastry – or for a lighter dish, buy filo. Place 12 oz (300 g)
salmon fillets or 1 lb (400 g) salmon steaks in a pan, just
cover with water. Add 1 sliced carrot, 1 sliced celery stick
and a bouquet garni. Bring to the boil slowly and poach
very gently for 5 minutes. Remove the fish from the pan,
strain the stock and set aside. Sauté 1 large chopped onion
in 1 tablespoon oil until soft. To this, add 4 oz (100 ml) of
rice that has been cooked in salted water till tender and
drained, and stir well. Set aside.*

*Meanwhile, prepare a duxelle of mushrooms by sautéeing
¼ lb (100 g) very finely chopped mushrooms and 1 finely
chopped shallot in 1 tablespoon of butter. Add salt, pepper
and 2 tablespoons white wine and cook until most of the
moisture has evaporated. Add 1 tablespoon of single cream
and cook until the mixture is thick. Remove and set aside.*

*Flake the salmon and remove all the bones, then assemble
the coulibiac: Divide the pastry in half and roll out into
2 oblongs, one piece approximately 10″ × 8″ (25 cm ×
20 cm), the other piece slightly larger. Place the larger oblong
on a baking tray and spread with mushroom duxelle to*

within 1 inch of the edge of the pastry. Then, spread over half the flaked salmon, all the rice, then the other half of the salmon, then the mushroom duxelle. Dampen the edges of both pieces of pastry with water and place the smaller piece over the mixture. Press to seal the pieces together. Make three diagnonal slashes along the top of the pastry to allow steam to escape while cooking, and brush with milk. Cook in a preheated oven at 425 °F/220 °C/Gas Mark 7 for about 30 minutes, making sure that the top doesn't burn.

This makes a wonderful supper dish served with sour cream. It is not a dish for dieters, but a less calorific version can be created, replacing the pastry with blanched lettuce leaves.

Coulis

Formerly the term for the juices which escaped from fish or meat during cooking, a coulis now indicates a puréed sauce, usually of vegetables, herbs or fruit, which is served as an accompaniment to a fish dish. You will often find fish or shellfish served on top of a coulis of red peppers, or **tomatoes** or mango. A stunning Sydney dish is concocted with steamed **scallops** served on a coulis of lettuce: *Cook the lettuce in salted water for 2 minutes, rinse in iced water, dry it and purée in a blender or push through a sieve. Then add a little fish* **stock**, *nutmeg and a little cream. Heat gently and serve beneath the scallops.*

Court-bouillon

This is the liquid used for poaching fish or shellfish, usually made by simmering vegetables, herbs and seasoning in water, wine or in a mixture of water and wine, or in a mixture of water with vinegar added, or milk. If fish trimmings are added to this it becomes fish **stock**; if it is reduced by boiling to become a much more strongly flavoured liquid it becomes a fish **fumet**, which makes an excellent base for a fish sauce. *A basic court-bouillon should look something like this: 4 pints (2½ litres) of cold water, ½ pint (3 dl) of white wine, 2 tablespoons wine vinegar or lemon juice, one medium sliced onion, one medium sliced carrot, 2 stalks chopped celery, 4 parsley leaves with stalks, 1 tablespoon salt, 1 teaspoon whole peppercorns, a bay leaf, 2 sprigs of fresh thyme or ½ teaspoon dried thyme. Bring to the boil and simmer for 30 minutes, before straining ready for poaching fish. You can vary quantities here (add more or less wine or vinegar as desired) and add different herbs – though be careful with sage and rosemary – they are a little strong for the delicate flavour of fish.*

Some fish, such as haddock and most smoked fish, are better in a milk court-bouillon which is simply milk or equal quantities of milk and water with a teaspoon of lemon juice, salt and black pepper. The milk, once it has been used for poaching, makes a good base for a **sauce** or a fish **pie**.

Crab   L   84 crabe/crustacean

There were, at the last count, 4,400 different kinds of crab – and they are all edible. The crab you will most often find in the UK is the Common Crab or Brown Crab, which is, when fresh, a dull brown. Crabs do not turn pink until they have been boiled.

While it is easier to buy a dressed crab (one where the crab meat has been removed, mashed up with the crab's liver, a little oil, mustard and seasoning and then replaced in the shell), an un-dressed but cooked crab represents a considerable saving. When buying an undressed crab, buy on heaviness in the hand rather than size – a large lightweight one may prove to be rather hollow.

To extract the meat from a cooked crab:
1 Lay the crab on its back and remove the apron – the T-shaped or triangular segment on the underside of the crab.
2 Pull off the carapace, or top shell, by gripping it firmly in the gap left by the apron and pulling sharply upwards.
3 Twist off the two large claws where they join the body, crack them open and extract meat, then do the same with the legs.
4 Remove the gills (often called dead men's fingers) from either side.
5 Cut off the 'face' of the crab about ½ inch behind the eyes.
6 With your fingers snap the body in half, and, with a small knife, pick meat out.

To dress a crab: Place the white meat and the brown meat in separate bowls. Mix the brown meat with 1 tablespoon of mayonnaise, and salt and black pepper to taste. Spoon this mixture into the centre of the washed and dried crab shell. Flake the white meat and arrange it on either side of the brown. Garnish with a little chopped egg yolk, chopped egg white and sprinkle with a little chopped parsley. Cooked crab makes an attractive addition to a summer salad; is a quick and easy starter when teamed with avocado and lime mayonnaise, and can be mixed with a plain white fish, like **whiting** to make a tasty terrine. A crab **soufflé** cooked and served in the shell makes an impressive starter.

Crawfish   L   110 langouste/crustacean

Also known as the spiny lobster, the crawfish is a reddish-brown rough-shelled lobster which is considered to be the most desirable of all crustaceans – a fact reflected in its price and availability. Treat as **lobster**.

Crayfish   L   87 ecrevisse/crustacean

Small, grey freshwater crayfish with red claws, which turn bright pink when boiled. More common in France, where they poach them in a white wine **court-bouillon** or use them as a garnish for other fish dishes. If you are lucky enough to get hold of any, treat them as **prawns**.

Creole

A style of cooking that originated in the southern States of North America, and which is currently in vogue, thanks to a renewed interest in ethnic foods in the US. The signature ingredients of Creole dishes are tomatoes, peppers and onions, which are all included in Seafood **Gumbo** and Seafood Jambalaya. New Orleans' most famous recipe for Seafood Jambalaya includes white fish fillets, oysters, prawns, smoked sausage, smoked ham, tomatoes, green peppers, red peppers and rice.

Crêpe

Thin crêpes or pancakes are ideal for filling with a fish and shellfish mixture, rolled up and served with a mornay **sauce** well garnished with chopped parsley. *For a simple seafood crêpe: Make a pancake batter from 4 oz (100 g) white flour, 4 oz (100 g) wholewheat flour, a pinch of salt, 3 eggs, ½* *pint (3 dl) milk, 3 tablespoons water mixed together (ideally in a blender) until thick, creamy and lump-free. Refrigerate for 2 hours before use. Brush a 7" fry pan with a little oil and place over a moderately high heat. Pour about 2 tablespoons of the mixture into the pan and spread it evenly. Cook for about a minute then flip it. Stack the cooked crêpes in a pile, separating each one with greaseproof paper, so they don't stick. Set aside. For the filling: First make a thick béchamel* **sauce** *with 2 tablespoons butter, 2 oz (50 g) of flour, and 1 pint (6 dl) milk, salt and pepper, a grating of nutmeg and a dash of lemon juice and set aside. Then melt 1 tablespoon of butter in a pan, soften 1 finely chopped shallot (about 1 tablespoon) for a minute then add 1 lb (400 g) of cooked and flaked mixed white fish and shellfish —whiting or cod for instance, cooked mussels, cooked shrimps or prawns – this is ideal for leftovers. Stir well over a medium heat until heated through, then add half of the béchamel sauce and mix well. Lay the crêpes out on a work surface and prepare a buttered baking tin. Divide the filling between the crêpes, roll them up and place in the baking tin. Add 2 tablespoons grated cheese to the remaining béchamel. Heat and stir till cheese is dissolved then spoon the sauce over the crêpes. Sprinkle with a further tablespoon of grated cheese, a few dots of butter and cook for about 10 minutes in a pre-heated oven at 425 °F/220 °C/Gas Mark 7 for about 10 minutes, till the top is golden brown. Serve sprinkled with chopped parsley.*

Croquette   HC

Cooked and flaked fish mixed with seasoning, milk, egg and breadcrumbs, formed into small sausage shapes, rolled in dried breadcrumbs and deep-fried: *Finely mince 1 lb (400 g) cooked, flaked fish (any white fish will do), making sure all*

*bones and the skin have been removed, together with 1 lb
(400 g) cooked roughly chopped potato, 1 chopped fennel
bulb (replace with 1 chopped onion, softened slightly in
butter, if fennel is not available), 1 chopped clove of garlic,
3 tablespoons chopped parsley, 2 eggs, 1 tablespoon of
butter, 2 tablespoons of white wine or fish stock, salt and
fresh ground black pepper. Make sure all the ingredients are
well blended and set aside for an hour in the refrigerator to
firm. Shape into croquettes, roll in either breadcrumbs or,
for a more interesting flavour, sesame seeds, until well-
coated and cook in a pan with a little oil, until golden on all
sides.* If you want to use cooked fish in a simple supper
dish, try grilled **fishcakes** and avoid the deep-frying.

Croûte

Croûte is the French word for crust. En croûte usually means
wrapped in pastry, but with fish you can try substituting
much lighter wrappings such as filo pastry, **spinach** leaves,
lettuce leaves, or **vine** leaves. Whole fish can be wrapped in
a crust of rock **salt** or topped with a herb crust, as in sea
bass en croûte.

Croûtons

Small pieces of fried bread served with Soupe de Poissons,
and scattered over fish served with Sauce **Grenobloise**.

Crudités

These are raw vegetables such as thin slivers of carrots,
celery, red and green peppers, courgettes and cucumber, plus
fleurettes of cauliflower and broccoli, often served in an attractive arrangement as a first course with a dip, such as **Aïoli**
or **Bagna Cauda**.

Cucumber   10

Cucumber is such a pretty fresh vegetable that is is traditionally associated with the things of summer – like cold
poached salmon or trout, salmon and cucumber mousse, or
cucumber and prawns in little aspic moulds. Chopped up
with fresh chervil or dill or even parsley and blended with
homemade or low-calorie **mayonnaise** it makes an attractive
pale green sauce for almost any cold fish or shellfish dish. *A
cucumber sauce for weight watchers: Mix ½ pint (3 dl)
yoghurt (or half yoghurt and half low-calorie mayonnaise),
1 tablespoon of white wine, the juice of ½ lime (or lemon),
with a 4 inch piece of peeled and finely diced cucumber, and
1 tablespoon of chopped dill, chervil or parsley, with salt
and black pepper to taste.* Cucumber can be braised in small
cubes in just a little butter and used hot as a garnish for a
plain grilled or poached fish. It can also be added to a fish
stuffing: *Cook 1 finely chopped onion in a little butter till
soft, then mix in a bowl with 6 oz (150 g) soft breadcrumbs,
a 4 inch piece of cucumber peeled and finely diced, 1 tablespoon of parsley, 1 teaspoon thyme, ½ teaspoon sage, the
juice and zest of 1 lime or lemon, and salt and pepper to
taste. Mix all the ingredients together and bind with 1 egg.*

Curry

A very light curry sauce can add interest and spice (without
hotness) to a bland fish. If you have only frozen cod in the
house, a gentle curry sauce could turn it into a mild but interesting supper dish: *Finely chop 1 onion and 1 small garlic clove
in 2 teaspoons of butter and sweat over a low heat till
translucent. Remove from heat and mix in 2 teaspoons curry
powder, ¼ teaspoon powdered ginger, and a pinch of saffron. Return to a low heat, then slowly add ½ pint (3 dl)*

yoghurt, and heat, but do not boil. Serve over cod poached or baked in foil. For a cold curry sauce to use as a seafood dip; Add 1 teaspoon of curry powder and a little grated onion to ½ pint (6 dl) **mayonnaise.**

Fish and Vegetable Curry: It is the chillies that make this fish and vegetable curry hot – if you are looking for a mild curry, omit the fresh chillie but leave in the chillie powder: *Poach 1 lb (440 g) white fish fillets such as coley in ½ pint (300 ml) water along with 1 sliced carrot, ½ sliced onion, 6 black peppercorns and a sprig of parsley, for about 5 mins, or until tender. Remove fish from stock. When cool, remove skin and bones, break the fish into large flakes, and set aside.*

   Meanwhile, in a large heavy-bottomed pan, sauté 1½ finely sliced onions in 2 tablespoons oil, until soft and golden. Raise the heat, add 1 inch peeled and grated fresh root ginger, 2 cloves crushed garlic, 2 tablespoons crushed coriander seeds, 1 teaspoon mustard seeds, ½ teaspoon chillie powder and stir well for 2 minutes. Then add 1 diced potato, 1 finely chopped green chillie, 4 peeled and seeded chopped tomatoes, and ½ lb (200 g) of chopped mushrooms. Stir well, then add the fish stock (bringing up to ½ pint (3 dl) if necessary with a little water or wine, or with a mixture of the two). Cover, bring to the boil and simmer gently for 10 minutes or until the potato is soft. Add flaked fish and 2 teaspoons garam masala. Heat through and serve with rice.

Cuttlefish   [L] 96 seiche/cephalopod

First cousin of the squid, usually around eight to ten inches in length. Cuttlefish can be stuffed, braised, sautéed or even grilled, and looks stunning when served with a thick rich jet-black sauce made from the ink in its sac: *Carefully remove the ink sacs from 2 cuttlefish and set aside in a small bowl. Sweat a finely chopped shallot in a little butter in a high-sided pan over a medium heat. Add the ink sacs and chop in with the shallots. Take care the ink doesn't squirt out of the pan: it can be hard to remove. Add a glass of white wine and stir, reducing the liquid by half. Add a little fish stock and 2 tablespoons of single cream to get a thick, even consistency. It will appear pale grey at first but will gradually turn jet-black. Season to taste and add a little lemon juice. Sieve and set aside.*

Cut cleaned cuttlefish (see **squid** *for cleaning details) into strips or squares. In a pan, heat 1 chopped clove of garlic in a little oil. Remove garlic and add the cuttlefish, sautéeing over a high heat for about 1 minute. Return the garlic to the pan, and stir quickly for 1 minute, then remove from heat. Heat the ink sauce with a small knob of butter, pour on to individual plates and arrange the cuttlefish on top of the sauce.* In fashionable pasta circles cuttlefish ink is now used to make black pasta, which is sometimes served with steamed shellfish, especially scallops.

Dab

A small flat fish with very rough scales, looking something like a sole. More highly thought of in France than it is here even though it is much less expensive on this side of the channel. Small fresh dabs can be skinned then grilled whole like a small plaice or small lemon sole, and served with a savoury **butter** – something simple like lemon butter or parsley butter. Larger dabs should be filleted and treated like **plaice**.

Darne

A thick slice of fish, especially of salmon, cut horizontally like a fish steak, but not quite as thick. It can be grilled, poached, braised or cooked en papillote.

Dashi

Japanese fish stock. This can be bought in powder form or made from **dried fish**.

Dill

Dill is probably Scandinavia's favourite herb. They use it in all sorts of fish dishes, fish sauces and in their famed **Gravad Lax**, which is becoming increasingly popular world-wide. Dill is extremely versatile and works well with a wide range of fish. With parsley and lemon it makes a pretty dill **butter**; with white wine, mixed with shallots and yoghurt, it becomes a very fresh tasting warm sauce: *In a pan, reduce 12 tablespoons fresh chopped dill and 1 tablespoon of finely chopped spring onion in ½ pint (3 dl) white wine until it is half its volume. Slowly add ½ pint (3 dl) yoghurt, 1 teaspoon of lemon juice and salt and pepper to taste. Press through a sieve or mix in blender and serve warm. If the mixture tastes too sharp, add a little brown sugar, or sweetener.* Dill mixes marvellously with mustard. Make a dill and mustard sauce to serve with **Gravad Lax**, cold fish or shellfish by mixing: *1 tablespoon of chopped dill (1 teaspoon of dried dill) with 1½ tablespoons of French mustard and ½ pint (3 dl) mayonnaise (remember to use half low-cal mayonnaise and half yoghurt if you are counting calories).* And mixed together with watercress, chives, tarragon and parsley (or any similar fresh green herb) in a mayonnaise base it makes a very attractive **green sauce** for cold fish dishes.

For a very simple salmon dish: *wrap salmon steaks in foil with salt, pepper, lemon juice, 1 teaspoon of white wine and a generous sprig of dill and bake according to the* **Canadian Theory.**

Dogfish   O 178 petite roussette/round

Also known as catfish, huss, flake, rigg. More commonly sold in the UK as rock salmon (because of its salmony-pink flesh) or rock eel. A member of the shark family, dogfish is much favoured by the nation's fish-friers, but it can be cut into chunks and used as an inexpensive 'filler' to a fish soup or a fish stew made with a mixture of rock salmon, any lean white fish, wine, peppers, tomatoes, onions and garlic: *Cut 1 lb (400 g) fish into chunks, flour lightly and brown in a little olive oil together with plenty of crushed garlic (2 cloves should be enough), and 1 chopped onion. Then add 1 small green chopped pepper, 1 × 15 oz (375 g) tin tomatoes and white wine, 1 tablespoon chopped tarragon or basil and 1 tablespoon parsley and simmer for 15 minutes.*

Dover Sole   102 sole/lean, flat

Considered the king of the flat white fish. Its price reflects its lofty status. It has a firm, white flesh with such a delicate flavour that it is possibly at its best served plain grilled (remove the rough upper skin) with a squeeze of fresh lime. If you must have a sauce, keep it simple – something like a lime hollandaise **sauce**, served to the side not on top. However, for those who insist on gilding the lily, Larousse, in his *Encyclopaedia Gastronomique*, lists one hundred and three different ways of preparing sole, ranging from Sole à l'Americaine (where the sole is sautéed in olive oil, wine, brandy and tomatoes, garnished with slices of fresh lobster and served with an Americaine sauce made from the coral and liver of lobster sautéed in butter, then mashed), to Sole Waleska (where the sole is poached in a **fumet**, garnished with truffles and a slice of lobster, and covered with a mornay **sauce**). Large dover soles can be **filleted** like any flat fish.

Dried Fish

The Japanese use dried **bonito** to mix with dried seaweed
and a little soy sauce and water to make **dashi**, a fish stock:
*Prepare 1 oz (25 g) of dried bonito, grated or flaked, 1 oz
(25 g) of seaweed, and 2 pints of water. Bring to the boil,
simmer and strain and, if desired, add a teaspoon of soy
sauce.* All the ingredients are available at oriental delicatessens, but may be hard to find outside the main city
centres.

Dublin Bay Prawn   L 120 langoustine/shellfish

Popularly known as scampi in the UK and as langoustines
in France, the correct name for the Dublin Bay Prawn is the
Norway Lobster (which, incidentally, has no geographical
links with Dublin Bay). Norway lobsters were once sold in
Dublin in large quantities by street-vendors like Molly
Malone. They look like small lobsters with long claws and
are bright pink before and after boiling. Capture the taste of
very fresh ones by brushing them lightly with olive oil and
lemon juice, threading them on to a skewer, and grilling or
barbequing. Peel as **prawns**.

Duxelle

A mixture of **mushrooms** and onions or shallots, cooked
together until soft, which is often used in a **stuffing** or as a
base for fish during **braising**: *In about 1 tablespoon of butter
or fish* **fumet***, sweat 4 oz (100 g) finely chopped mushrooms
(including stalks) with 4 oz (100 g) finely chopped onion or
shallot, until soft.*

Eel Anguille

Provided it is not too fatty, the freshwater eel can be quite deliciously sweet when cut into steaks, marinated gently in a little oil, wine and lemon juice then grilled, or, even better, casseroled slowly in red wine to which has been added softened chopped onion and garlic, and a good quantity of full-flavoured herbs (especially rosemary): *Sauté 1 chopped onion, 1 carrot and 1 leek in 2 tablespoons butter. Add 1 bottle red wine, 1 teaspoon rosemary, 2 sprigs parsley, 1 tablespoon thyme and a bay leaf, and simmer gently for 1 hour. Meanwhile, in a separate saucepan, sauté 12 baby onions in 1 tablespoon butter. Remove and in the same pan, lightly sear 1½ lbs (600 g) bite-sized pieces of skinned eel. Add 1 fl oz (25 ml) of cognac, stir, then add the eels to the sauce. Simmer for about 20 minutes, thicken with a few small pieces of* **beurre manié**, *add the button onions, sprinkle with parsley and serve.*

Eels are difficult to skin, so try to persuade your fishmonger to do it for you. If he won't, the best advice is to tie a piece of string tightly around the head of the eel and suspend the string from a hook so that you can reach it easily. Slit the skin right around just below the head and peel it back so that you can get a good grip. Either with well-salted fingers or a pair of pliers, work the skin downwards, pulling it off like a tight pair of gloves.

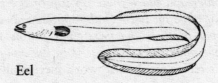

Eel

Eel is becoming increasingly popular smoked and served with a horseradish sauce or a spicy apple sauce as a simple but effective starter. The calorie count can vary quite considerably in eels – from 190 to 230 – depending on the fat content.

Elver   [L] 198 Anguille/round, oily

This is the young eel, usually about 3 years old, returning to its river habitat from the sea. Regarded as a delicacy in some parts of Europe – treat as **whitebait**, but wash them well in salted water first to remove the slimy coating.

En Papillote

The French term for baking in a sealed foil or paper parcel. See **foil**.

Escabeche

A cold, cooked and marinated fish dish, popular in West Africa, the Caribbean, Latin America and now becoming a Pacific Cuisine regular. In Sydney an Escabeche of Sea Trout served on a watercress salad featured: *4 fillets of trout weighing about 5 or 6 oz (125–150 g) each, seasoned with a little sea salt and a sprinkling of fresh chopped herbs. Seal in a little heated olive oil over a medium heat, but don't cook through. Remove the fish from the pan, and place with herbs in a deep dish. Slice 6 large, ripe tomatoes, and chop 1 small cucumber and place these on top of the trout. Mix ½ pint (3 dl) of olive oil with 4 tablespoons red wine vinegar and pour over the fish and vegetables. Allow to marinate overnight and serve on salad tossed in the vinaigrette from the fish.* This recipe would also work successfully with rainbow trout.

A Los Angeles version uses sun-dried tomatoes to give a much fuller flavour to the Escabeche marinade. Elsewhere in California, red and green peppers are included in the marinade mix, and south of the border they add hot red chillies.

Fennel

Fish and fennel have been going together for a very long time. Shakespeare talked of the pleasures of conger eel and fennel. A herb and vegetable with a slight anise flavour, the fennel is thrice favoured: Firstly, for its bulbous stem, which is sliced or diced and used in **stuffings** or as a 'bed', especially with red mullet, or red snapper. Secondly, for its leaves, which are used as a chopped herb to sprinkle inside and outside fish being baked or cooked en papillote or in **foil**. And thirdly, for its dried seeds, which can be used to flavour **sauces** and stuffings in the absence of fresh fennel. Fennel **butter** is a deliciously simple way of dressing up a baked or grilled bream or snapper. Chopped fresh fennel bulb will need to be softened for about a minute in enough boiling water to cover it, before being mixed with the softened butter. And, at only 6 calories per oz (25 g), fennel won't do too much harm to your diet.

If you are growing your own fennel and have plenty of it, dry the stems and toss them on your barbeque whenever you are grilling fish. Incidentally there are two fennels: the very common sweet perennial fennel, which is the tall, feathery one with the yellow flowers; and the more versatile and much to be preferred Florence fennel, which looks like a short version of celery with a round bottom. Apparently, the Florence fennels with rounder, flatter bottoms are the female fennels and have a sweeter taste than the male.

Filleting

Your fishmonger will generally fillet your fish for you (if not, change fish shops), but if you are landed with a whole fish and decide you would rather have fillets than a whole fish, here's how to tackle it:

ROUND FISH

A round fish like a trout or a mackerel should be cleaned and gutted first. Then make a slit across the fish immediately below the head as deep as the backbone but not cutting through the bone (see diagram). Turn knife flat and, lying it on top of the backbone, work it towards the tail with smooth, slicing strokes, freeing the flesh from the backbone. When you reach the tail, twist the knife upwards to cut off the fillet. Turn the fish over and repeat the process.

If you want to 'butterfly' the fish; that is, to have the two fillets joined but opened flat in a shape vaguely reminiscent of a butterfly; cut off the head of the fish and work down both sides of the backbone, as above. Then, instead of cutting the fillet at the tail, carefully pull out the backbone, and open out the fish. You will need to make a small incision at either side of the tail and remove the tail leaving a V-shape to get it to lie flat.

To skin the fillets, salt your fingers and grasp the fillet by the tail end, in your left hand (assuming you are right-handed). Cut through the fillet as deep as the skin but not through the skin. With the knife blade flat against the fillet,

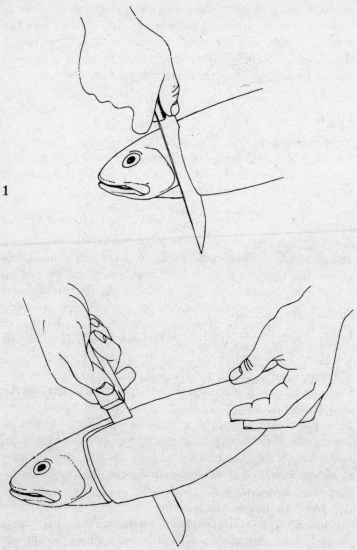

1

2

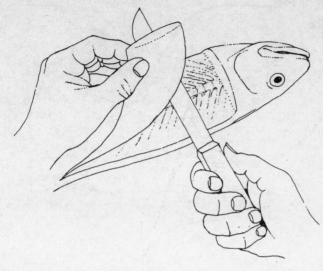

3

Filleting a round fish:

1 Cut across the fish and slice down gently until the knife presses against the bone structure.
2 With smooth, slicing strokes, run the knife along the length of the fish, pressing the knife flat against the bone structure.
3 Repeat on the other side of the fillet, so that the whole fillet is freed from the bone structure.

work the knife away from you between the fillet and the skin as close to the skin as possible, gradually pulling the skin free (see diagram).

If you are serving your fillets flat make little slits at 1 inch intervals around the edge of the fillet or it will curl up during cooking.

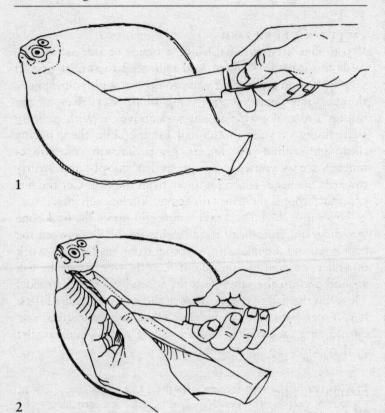

1

2

Filleting a flat fish:

1 To produce 4 fillets, place the fish dark side up on a cutting
  board and slice down the centre as deep as the backbone from
  head to tail.

2 Starting at the head end, insert the knife between the
  backbone and the flesh. Lifting the flesh as you cut, make
  short, slicing strokes from head to tail, then cut the fillet free.
  Repeat on the same side for the second fillet, then turn the
  fish over to prepare another two fillets.

FILLETING FLAT FISH

If you have a large flat fish like a plaice or sole which you wish to turn into 4 fillets, you will need to skin it first. If you are reasonably strong you can do this with your fingers, though some people prefer to use small pliers. Cut off the tail-fin and make a small slit just above it. With either a sharp knife or your thumb-nail lift the skin, then, having thoroughly salted your fingers, grasp the skin and with as much force as you can muster, pull it sharply and swiftly towards the head, tearing it away from the fish. Cut the fins off right around the fish with strong kitchen scissors.

To remove the fillets, make a cut right down the backbone (see diagram) from head to tail. Slide the blade between the backbone and the fillet and, working from head to tail, work one fillet (i.e. half of one side of the fish) free. Turn the fish around and do the same with the second fillet on that side. Then flip the fish over and remove the two remaining fillets. If you then wanted to make your fillets into **paupiettes**, you should beat them lightly with a rolling pin or small mallet so they will keep their shape.

Finnan Haddie |O| 115 haddock/smoked, round

Haddocks, originally smoked over peat in the fishing village of Findan on the north-east coast of Scotland. Now this is a general term for a superior smoked haddock. Smoking does not increase the calories in fish, but there have been suggestions – yet to be proved – that too much smoked fish may not be beneficial because of substances that may be involved in the smoking process.

Finnan Haddie can be served as a breakfast treat – with rice and hard-boiled eggs it becomes **kedgeree** (an Anglicization of the Hindu spiced rice dish khichri); mixed with other **smoked fish**, it is transformed into a sophisticated

supper dish; poached and crumbled, it is used in the classic
Omelette Arnold Bennet; or it can be used raw in a **tartare**
of smoked haddock or poached, cooled and flaked in a refreshing **Waldorf** salad.

Fins

Remove fins using kitchen scissors to cut them off at the
base. Pull out any fin-bones remaining with fingers or
tweezers. If you are cooking the fish with the skin on, make
sure you don't tear the skin while removing fins.

Fishcakes   HC   O

A great late-night supper dish, fishcakes can be made with
almost any cooked flaked fish, combined with either potato
or breadcrumbs, seasoned with herbs, bound with a beaten
egg, then moulded into patties, brushed with a little oil and
cooked under a hot grill. One of London's smartest late-
night restaurants makes great salmon fishcakes with
poached flaked fresh salmon, mashed potato, mustard and
Worcester sauce and serves them with a sorrel sauce – the
perfect after-theatre dish when you don't want anything too
rich or heavy. For simple salmon fishcakes: *Skin, bone and
flake 12 oz (300 g) cooked salmon with 12 oz (300 g) well-
seasoned mashed potatoes, 1 tablespoon of grated onion, 1
teaspoon of minced garlic, 2 tablespoons of finely chopped
parsley, and, if you have it, 1 teaspoon of fresh finely
chopped dill. Combine well, and beat in 1 large egg to bind.
Form into large patties, flour lightly, and sauté in a little
butter or oil until golden on each side and cooked through.
Serve with sorrel sauce, dill sauce or fresh tomato sauce and
a sprig of fresh parsley.* High in Omega 3 and fibre, but not
quite the perfect slimmer's supper. However, grilling the

fishcakes would slightly reduce that high calorie rating.

The Alaska Seafood Marketing Bureau, faced with a surplus of salmon, recently created their version of the fishcake, which they called, naturally, a salmon burger. It combined cold poached salmon, flaked, finely chopped onions, wholemeal breadcrumbs, an egg, lemon juice, a little dried rosemary, and salt and pepper, well-mixed then formed into patties, lightly brushed with oil and grilled over charcoal.

Flambé

A dish sprinkled with spirits, most frequently brandy, and set alight before serving. Not a technique often used in fish cookery, though there is one interesting suggestion that flambéing oily fish with gin helps to cut the oiliness.

Flat Fish

The general name for flat oval fish such as dab, plaice, lemon sole, dover sole, brill, turbot and halibut.

Flounder   L   102 flet/flat

A mottled-brown oval flat fish of a similar taste and texture to a plaice, though not quite so tasty. It has a fairly delicate flavour (some would say bland) so it needs to be cooked with care. Grill it whole only if it is very fresh, otherwise poach it as fillets and serve with a fairly sharp sauce such as sorrel, or bake in foil with plenty of lemon juice and chopped herbs. Treat as plaice or lemon sole.

Fluke

Another name for flounder.

Foil

Cooking in foil sounds much more glamorous in French –
they call it 'en papillote', describing the butterfly shape the
foil should make before it is sealed (see diagram). It is
probably the easiest and most effective way of cooking fish
and retaining its full flavour without drying it out. You will
be surprised what 1 tablespoon of wine and 1 teaspoon of
chopped herbs, some salt and fresh black pepper can do to a
piece of fish, once they've spent some time together wrapped
in the same piece of foil in your oven. You can use foil
cooking for fish fillets, fish steaks or whole fish.

There are several important factors to remember when
baking in foil (in the absence of foil, you can use greaseproof
paper):

1   Make sure you cut a large enough piece of foil to
   allow room for any vegetables you may include on,
   under or around the fish plus room for the packet to
   rise with the steam generated within.
2   First, fold the foil in half.
3   Cut the foil into a semi-circle as in diagram.
4   Brush the foil lightly with butter or oil.
5   Place fish, vegetables, seasoning, herbs, wine or **fumet**
   in the centre of the foil.
6   Seal it with very tight edges so that no steam or liquids
   can escape.
7   Be careful to leave plenty of space inside the packet,
   or the steam and the aromas will not be able to move
   around the fish during cooking.
8   Place the foil packages in a baking dish or on a baking
   tray just in case they do leak.
9   Extract parcels from oven very carefully so they do
   not puncture.
10   Cook according to the **Canadian Theory**, but add 5
   minutes more for foil.

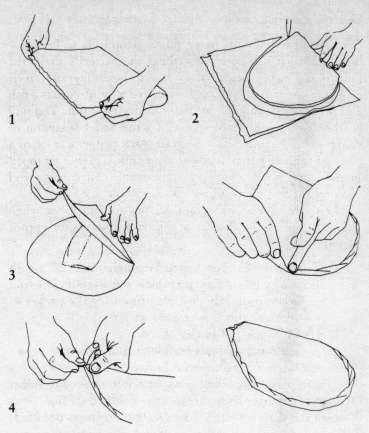

Cooking with foil:

1 Fold the sheet of foil in half.
2 Cut it into the shape of half a heart, or half a circle.
3 Unfold the foil and lay the fish on one half, near the fold. Add seasoning, herbs, a splash of wine or lemon juice and fold the foil over the fish.
4 Press the ends of the foil together and fold over twice so that the package is completely sealed. Place on a baking tray or in a baking dish.

You may want to remove fish from their parcels and pour the vegetables and juices over them before serving, or you may want to serve everybody with their own parcels and let them have the pleasure of slitting them open themselves and getting first whiff of the wonderful aroma inside. A simple dish like lemon sole with lemon-grass cooked in individual foil packages provides such an exotic aroma that it should always be slit at the table.

When it comes to calorie-conscious cooking, fish and foil are a dieter's best friend. It is possible to cook a piece of fish in foil without adding any extra calories – simply sprinkle the fish with salt and ground black pepper (no calories) and a teaspoon of fresh lime juice or lemon juice (no calories). Wrap in foil, seal, and bake for approximately 15 minutes. You could go over the top and add a pinch of ginger to the lime juice which would cost you almost a calorie (an eighth of a teaspoon of ground ginger equals 1 calorie).

Freezing

Never re-freeze fish that has been frozen and thawed. Make sure fresh fish is cleaned, gutted and scaled before wrapping it twice in plastic film, or in two plastic freezer bags – just in case the first one should tear. Date fish and do not freeze longer than three months; because of the high oil content, fish tends to oxidize and turn rancid much more quickly than meat or poultry. Only freeze cooked fish if it is immersed in a sauce – though cooked shellfish such as prawns and shrimps can be frozen. The Massachusetts Division of Marine Fisheries suggest that a better method of freezing fresh fish is to place the fish in a covered, plastic freezer container filled with lightly-salted water and then freeze it. Once frozen the fish is protected by a solid block of ice which can be thawed when needed.

Fritters

HC

Batter with fish or, more commonly, shellfish mixed in and lightly fried in oil or butter; obviously not a dish for dieters. In New Zealand during the whitebait season, many restaurants serve the most delicious **whitebait fritters**, which are really more of a whitebait omelette and cooked in just a little butter.

Frozen Fish

Of course fresh tastes best, but there are many times when you are miles from the coast or any source of fresh fish, so then you have to settle for frozen. Better frozen fish than no fish, especially with today's sophisticated freezing techniques. Fish can be cooked straight from the freezer if necessary – simply double the time i.e. 20 minutes per inch instead of 10. Oily fish, such as salmon, work better cooked from frozen than leaner kinds of fish, like plaice or cod.

Frying

Frying has been defined as a method of cooking food in hot fat. In terms of your health and your waistine, it is the worst thing you can do with fish. Deep-frying in oil almost trebles the calorific value of any fish and can clog up your arteries with saturated fats. However, there are many people who won't eat fish unless it is fried. If you have one of those in your family, or as a friend, and you have to deep-fry, use vegetable oil (sunflower, corn or peanut) and make sure that it is very hot – around the 375–400 °F/190–204 °C/Gas Mark 5–6. If the oil temperature is too low, the batter will take time to seal and will absorb a fair amount of fat, making it greasy and soggy on the plate.

To be deep-fried, fish must be coated in a batter, but if it is shallow-fried or pan-fried in a frying pan, it needs only to be coated lightly in flour. If you are pan-frying, you only need to coat the pan with a very thin layer of oil or butter – say ⅛ inch – but it should be at least 375 °F/190 °C/Gas Mark 5, so that the fish is sealed and doesn't soak up the fat. Shallow-frying and pan-frying are better for health and diet than deep-frying, but stir-frying, which uses either no fat or the absolute minimum of fat, is better still.

Fumet

A fish fumet is a fish **stock** that has been reduced in volume over a high heat so that it is much stronger and has much more flavour. It keeps well in the fridge or freezer once it has been strained, and is very useful as a base for fish sauces or for adding flavour to purées and coulis. If you cook a lot of fish always keep some handy – you can store it in empty yoghurt containers.

Garfish O 160 orphie/round

A slim, silvery fish with what appears to be a long thin beak, set with very sharp teeth, the garfish is also called needlenose and sea eel. Its bones – and they are many and fine – are a strange turquoise-blue, which probably gave rise to one suggestion (erroneous) that the garfish was poisonous. Traditionally, it is cut into small segments, floured and seasoned and then fried in butter, though the French sometimes bake it on a bed of sorrel, which helps to soften all those bones. It is a member of the eel family so use any eel recipe.

Garlic LC

Called a herb by some and a vegetable by others, garlic is reputed to have medicinal as well as aromatic powers. It is supposed to aid digestion, reduce fever, fight colds and keep the plague away. During the sixteenth century French doctors used to carry it so that they wouldn't catch their patients' ills.

In fish cookery it makes a world of difference to soups,

stews and many sauces, though it can be a little powerful for some delicate fish recipes. But strong fish like red mullet and red snapper love it. And the cold garlic sauce **Aïoli**, used as a dip for cold fish or shellfish will give you the very essence of Provence. For slimmers, garlic is guilt-free: there are no calories at all in a clove of garlic.

Always make sure that garlic is well minced. Either grind it in a mortar, crush it in a garlic press, or try the foil method: chop it quite finely, place it on a square of foil, add a little salt, fold up and crush with the back of a knife or a rolling pin. The simplest use of garlic is to make it into a garlic butter: *Mix together 3 or 4 cloves of peeled, blanched and minced garlic with a cup of softened butter. Form into a cylinder or roll, wrap in foil and chill for 3–4 hours. Cut off slices to decorate plain grilled or baked fish.* Or try roasting whole cloves of garlic with a large piece of fish, such as a large monkfish tail. If garlic cloves are cooked slowly they lose their sharpness and become quite deliciously sweet. If you are worried about the post-prandial after-effects, munch some fresh parsley.

Garnishes

In France if a dish is served garnished, it will usually include potatoes and perhaps a small portion of an appropriate vegetable. However, garnish in UK terms generally means the decorations used in presentation. This can get a little out of hand with some over-enthusiastic practitioners of nouvelle cuisine – the kiwi-fruit-with-everything brigade – so it is important to remember to keep garnishes striking but simple. Better a handful of chopped chives or fresh parsley sprinkled effortlessly but effectively over the fish, than three carefully sculpted, frilly-edged slices of truffle, placed exactly 3 centimetres apart from each other with military precision.

Because fish fillets are so often white, fresh green herbs – either a sprig, a couple of whole leaves, or a sprinkling of chopped herbs – always look stylish. Try dill or tarragon sprigs, whole leaves of basil or coriander or even mint. If the fish dish incorporates a herb, then try to use that herb as a garnish.

Lime (or lemon if you can't get lime) is always an attractive garnish. Sliced in very thin circles – or use the potato peeler to take long thin strips of lime peel and trim them into extra slim julienne strips to be tossed *seemingly* casually either in a small pile in the middle of the fish or scattered over the top. Similarly, use the peeler to take long thin vertical strips off spring onions – if these are thin enough they will curl up and look very attractive scattered on a whole fish. Or simply slice the spring onions in very thin circles and scatter them about. In the same way, you can also make julienne strips of red, green or yellow peppers – an effective garnish for cold fish dishes and salads, as long as it doesn't look too contrived.

Gazpacho

A spicy cold soup traditionally made from garlic, red and green peppers, cucumbers and tomatoes in chicken stock, which lends itself admirably to a fish conversion as in **Prawn** Gazpacho.

Gills

Gills are very useful to a fish – they couldn't breathe without them – but no use at all to the fish cook. They will leave a very bitter taste if kept in place during cooking, so remove them – even if you are planning to keep the head on. See diagram under **cleaning** to locate gill opening. The gills look like tiny concertinas.

Gin   50

Gin is not often used in fish cookery, but has on occasion been used to flambé oily fish, such as mackerel, herring or bluefish, to reduce the oil. Another suggested use was for poaching salmon: *Place salmon steaks in a pan with ⅛ pint (75 cl) of gin, fresh chopped parsley, a bay leaf, 6 black peppercorns, and enough water to cover. Serve with a watercress sauce made from the reduced gin-flavoured poaching liquid.*

Ginger   18

The Chinese used ginger in their fish cookery for generations before modern cooks caught on to the idea. Now, most fashionable restaurants have at least one dish boasting fresh ginger. It goes surprisingly well with salmon as well as with more delicate white fish like brill and sole, and makes a stunning combination with lime in a marinade for raw scallops. The lime and ginger combination also appears in a ginger and lime **butter** and a ginger and lime **vinaigrette**. Use fresh root ginger, cutting off a slice and chopping it very finely. Root ginger is not at all expensive and lasts a long time, powdered ginger does not have the same flavour. (Powdered ginger has 8 calories per teaspoon.)

Goatfish

Another name for **red mullet**.

Gooseberry   40

Traditionally, gooseberries are made into a sauce or a purée to be served with mackerel or herring; the sharpness of the gooseberry cutting the oiliness of the fish: *Simmer 1 lb (400 g) gooseberries in 1 oz (25 g) of butter until soft. Purée in a blender or put through a sieve and add 1 beaten egg, a dash of grated nutmeg and a little sugar if the gooseberries are very young and sharp. Because of the tartness of the sauce, a little goes a long way – this should serve 6–8.*

Goujons

These are small oblong pieces of fish, created by cutting slantwise across a flat fillet. The size and shape are meant to represent little gudgeons (tiny freshwater fish like smelts) which are usually served coated in egg and breadcrumbs and deep-fried.

Gratin

A gratin of fish is usually a dish of cooked fish that has been sprinkled with breadcrumbs and butter, or breadcrumbs and cheese, and browned in the oven. Smoked fish in a white wine sauce, or a cider sauce can be gratinéed to make a pleasant supper dish with a little parmesan cheese sprinkled on top of the breadcrumbs. Or you could try a gratin of mussels, brushing each mussel on the half shell with a little melted garlic butter, sprinkling them with breadcrumbs and browning them slightly under a very hot grill. See **Smoked Fish Gratinée**. Any dish with added cheese is likely to have a significantly higher calorie count.

Gravad Lax $\boxed{\text{O}}$

Also called Gravlax, this is a Scandinavian dish that means, literally, buried salmon – buried under a covering of dill, salt, sugar and peppercorns, and left to cure for 2 days. If you can persuade your fishmonger to prepare the fish for you – it needs to be scaled, but not skinned, boned and cut in half length-ways – it is a wonderfully easy and very impressive starter for a special dinner, or as a luncheon centrepiece: *If you have to prepare it yourself, follow the* **cleaning** *and* **boning** *instructions and, once you have bisected the fish, check both sides very carefully for tiny bones with a pair of tweezers. A 3 lb (1.2 kilo) fish will give you a good 1½ lb (600 g) edible Gravlax. At 4 oz (100 g) per person this should easily fill 6 people. Because it is so rich in flavour you would only need 2 oz (50 g) per person as a starter.*

The first time you try Gravad Lax it would be wise to experiment on a trout or a mackerel – Gravad Mac is a marvellous way to give a mackerel rather grand airs – or a small salmon tail. Once the fish is cleaned, boned and ready, place one half with the skin down in a large dish and mix together the following ingredients (these are for 3 lb (1½ kilo) fish); a large bunch of dill (about a dozen sprays, chopped); 2 tablespoons crushed white peppercorns; 2 tablespoons brown sugar; 4 tablespoons sea salt, and two tablespoons of brandy or, if you prefer, malt whisky. There is a delicious Gravad Lax produced on the banks of Loch Fyne in Scotland with malt whisky, and it goes without saying that a Gravad Mac would just have *to be made with whisky.*

Rub this mixture into the surface of the fish, making sure it is evenly covered. Place the other half of the fish on top of the covered half, making a sandwich with the dill mix in the middle. Wrap in foil. Place the fish beneath a weighted flat dish, plate, or even a small plank, and refrigerate, turning it every 12 hours or so for the next 2 days. To serve, scrape off the dill and salt mixture and slice it horizontally, with the blade almost flat against the fish surface, in long very thin slices like smoked salmon, decorated with a little fresh dill. It is traditionally served with a mustard and **dill** *sauce.*

Grayling $\boxed{O}$ 175 ombre/round

A type of freshwater trout with a firm white flesh. Treat as
trout.

Green Sauce

Attractive with cold poached fish. Green Sauce is **mayonnaise** with added spinach, watercress and green herbs such
as tarragon, parsley and chervil. Blanch herbs first, running
them under cold water so that they keep their colour, then
purée in a sieve or blender before straining and adding to
mayonnaise.

Grenobloise

A sauce used for flat fish such as sole, incorporating a little
melted butter, chopped capers, chopped parsley, lemon juice
and croûtons.

Grey Mullet $\boxed{O}$ 150 mulet/round

Not to be confused with that Mediterranean delight, the red
mullet, the grey mullet comes from a completely different
family. The one found most often in British waters is the
thick-lipped grey mullet, which can be recognized by the
small warts on the upper of its thick lips. Still good value
despite rising fish prices, it can be quite tasty provided it is
treated robustly enough to counteract a sometimes lack-
lustre flavour. Try it grilled with a strong savoury **butter**,
stuffed with a full-flavoured **stuffing**, or baked in a well-
flavoured liquid such as the white wine, olives and fennel
used for **whiting**.

Horseradish has the kind of flavour that will lift grey

mullet: *Make a savoury* **butter** *with softened butter mixed with either preserved horseradish or a little Japanese wasabi horseradish, which is available from oriental delicatessens. Make deep diagonal slashes across the grey mullet at 1 inch intervals and spread horseradish butter into these slashes. Place a little savoury butter inside the mullet, sprinkle with lemon juice, salt and pepper and place under a very hot grill, saving some savoury butter to brush on the fish when it is turned.*

Fresh ginger is also spicy enough to counteract grey mullet's potential blandness: *Clean, scale and gut a 2 lb (800 g) grey mullet, removing the gills but leaving the head. Slash the surface in a criss-cross diamond pattern and place in an ovenproof dish. Pour over 3 tablespoons sherry. Slice an inch long piece of root ginger very finely into thin slivers and place these in the slashes. Season well with salt and pepper. Cover and cook half through. Baste with sherry, then brush the fish with one dessertspoon soy sauce mixed with 1 dessertspoon olive oil. Cover and bake till ready, according to* **Canadian Theory**. The roes of grey mullet are used for an authentic **Taramasalata** or pressed into the exquisite but expensive **Botargo**.

Gribiche

A cold sauce featuring chopped hard-boiled eggs, capers, gherkins, parsley, tarragon, and chervil in a mayonnaise base to be served with cold fish or shellfish.

Grilling

Grilling is the perfect way to capture the flavour of very fresh fish, whether they are small whole round fish like sardines and herrings, whole flat fish like plaice or dover sole, fillets or steaks. Grilling is not only the simplest method of cooking fish, but, along with steaming, is one of the healthiest. Oily fish like mackerel, herrings and sardines are better suited to grilling than very lean fish. Slash them diagonally 2 or 3 times on each side, brush lightly with a little oil, sprinkle with salt and pepper, pop a few chopped herbs in the slashes, or even a little **mustard**, and grill on both sides according to the **Canadian Theory**. The fish should be translucent and will fall away from the bone when it is ready.

Flat fish (plaice, sole, etc) should be brushed with a little oil or clarified butter ($\frac{1}{2}$ a teaspoon of melted butter will suffice if you are dieting), seasoned and grilled on both sides. Fillets of fish can be brushed very lightly with flour before brushing with oil or butter and can be grilled on the fleshy side only to prevent breaking them in turning – though some people do like to brown the skin side slightly so that it is crisp. Grilling is probably the most effortless way of cooking fish, but here are some points to remember:

1 Pre-heat the grill to maximum and seal the juices in.
2 Brush the grilling rack with oil so that fish doesn't stick.
3 Place fish 2–4 inches from grill – no further.
4 Baste flat fish and fillets (and **brochettes**) during grilling.
5 Thin fillets may benefit from a little water underneath in the grill pan.
6 Fish steaks and brochettes can often be improved by marinating first.
7 Collect the grilling juices from the pan to pour over the fish, or into the accompanying sauce.

Grouper   L 116 mérou/round

Large heavy-jawed semi-tropical fish imported here from the warmer regions of the Mediterranean and increasingly from the Seychelles. One of the sea perch family, its firm, white flesh is ideal for cutting into steaks, to be grilled and served with a well-flavoured savoury **butter** such as basil and chive.

Gumbo

Seafood Gumbo is a Creole stew that usually contains the tomatoes and peppers that are the hallmark of Creole cooking, plus crab, prawns and shrimps, ham or bacon, garlic, and the essential gumbo ingredient, okra. Okra is a vegetable common to the Southern States of the US, Latin America and the West Indies, and is also known as Ladies' Fingers – presumably because of its long slender pods. There are some gumbo recipes that omit the ham and bacon. This red snapper and prawn gumbo uses bacon fat but this could be replaced by oil: *Heat 2 tablespoons bacon fat (or oil) in a saucepan, add ½ lb (200 g) okra, and cook for 10 minutes. Add 4 oz (100 g) tomato sauce and stir in well, continuing to cook until the mixture thickens slightly. In a separate large pot, heat a further 1 tablespoon bacon fat (or oil) and sprinkle in 2 tablespoons flour. Cook slowly over a low heat until golden brown. Add 8 oz (200 g) chopped onion, 2 stalks chopped celery, ½ chopped green pepper and 1 minced clove of garlic. Stir for a few minutes, cover and remove from the heat for about 10 minutes. Return to a low heat and add 1 pint (6 dl) water. Stir well, then allow to simmer for 3 minutes.*

Add a further ½ pint (3 dl) of water and leave to simmer for 20 minutes. Stir in the okra mixture. Add ½ lb (200 g) red snapper or red mullet fillets cut into bite-sized pieces (leave skin on) and 12 oz (300 g) peeled prawns. Season with salt, black pepper and 1–2 teaspoons cayenne pepper, depending on how hot you like your food. Cook for 10 minutes – or until fish and prawns are tender.

Gurnard

L 150 grondin/round

Grey or red with a large bony head and a long thin body, gurnard makes an odd grunting noise as it swims – as though it is snoring. It has dry, firm flesh that needs to be kept moist if baked. Otherwise, cut it into fillets, poach in stock; and reduce the stock to provide the base for a full-flavoured sauce, perhaps onion, fennel or tarragon. Gurnard is not at all expensive so it makes a good addition to fish soups such as **Bourride**.

Haddock L 83 aiglefin/round

This is first cousin to the cod, and is distinguishable by a dark patch below either gill, said to be another of St Peter's thumb-prints. Its firm, white flesh is considered superior to the cod (thus it is more expensive) because it is generally a little softer. It is neither firm enough nor tasty enough to grill, but it poaches well as long as it is then accompanied by a well-flavoured sauce. Useful in any dish requiring lean white fish, it can be substituted in any **cod** or **hake** recipes.

There is a German haddock recipe involving alternate layers of haddock, potatoes and onions baked in a sour cream and mustard sauce: *Rub 1½ lb (600 g) haddock fillets with salt and leave to stand for an hour. Lightly brown 2 thinly sliced onions in 1 oz (25 g) butter, and parboil (maximum ten minutes) 1 lb (400 g) potatoes. In a buttered casserole dish, place alternating layers of haddock fillets, potatoes and onions, sprinkling each layer with a little ground black pepper. Mix ½ pint (3 dl) sour cream or yoghurt with 2 beaten eggs and 2 oz (50 g) mustard and cook in a moderate oven, 375° F/190° C/Gas Mark 4, for 30 minutes*. By substituting yoghurt for the sour cream, you can reduce the calorie count.

Smoked haddock is often known as **finnan haddie**, and is also referred to in **smoked fish**.

Hake   [L]   84 merlu/round

Another cousin of the cod, with a tender, rather flaky white flesh which is sometimes described in France as saumon blanc – white salmon. Usually prepared in fillets or cutlets, it is especially popular in Portugal and Spain, where it is frequently poached in fish stock or wine then served in a green parsley **sauce**. Hake can also be steamed and served cold, on top of a mixed leaf salad and topped with herb **mayonnaise**. A hake steak is perfect for low-calorie foil-cooking with wine and herbs and works well with **microwave cooking**.

Hake

Halibut   [L]   105 flétan/flat

The largest of all the flat fish, halibut can grow up to 700 lbs in weight. Browny-black or greeny-black on its eye side and brilliant white on its blind side, the halibut has a tendency to dry out during cooking. It can be cut into steaks and grilled (though be careful to keep it moist by basting it); or baked in foil with a dab of butter, a generous grating of nutmeg, plenty of salt and pepper and a little wine, vermouth or fish stock to keep it from drying out. It can also be steamed or poached and served with a lightly-flavoured sauce. Halibut is becoming increasingly expensive, but it is quite a filling fish, so you don't need large portions. Any recipe for **turbot** or brill can be used for halibut.

Halibut

Herbs

Only five years ago the dried spice rack held pride of place in the kitchen. Now, with fresh herbs available in so many of the supermarkets for so much of the year, our dried herb dependency is much less acute. Don't throw your spice rack away though – there are times when fresh herbs are simply not available. But do experiment with growing one or two of your own, even if it is only a pot of basil or dill on your windowsill through the summer.

Some herbs are better than others with fish. Here is a list of those that flatter fish most: anise, basil, bay, chervil, chives, coriander, dill, fennel, garlic, lemongrass, marjoram, mint, parsley, sorrel, tarragon. All of these are listed individually.

Herbs to be used with discretion include: rosemary (which works only with very strongly flavoured fish like eel), sage (which should be used sparingly in stuffings), and thyme (which is ideal for a bouquet garni in stock or soup).

Herring   O 230 hareng/round

The name herring comes from the Teutonic word 'heer',

meaning an army, which is an apt description for the modus operandi of the herring, who frequently travel in shoals that are several miles wide. One of the best sources of Omega 3, herrings are an inexpensive treat when they are

Herring

really fresh. You can judge their freshness by their eyes, which should be very bright and protruding. They are at their best plain grilled (under a *very* hot grill) and served with a mustard **sauce**. Before grilling make 2 or 3 diagonal slashes in the skin and rub a little mustard sauce into each slash. Herrings also work well with a purée of **sorrel**, **gooseberry** sauce, or a tart apple sauce made from cooking apples, rather than sweet eating apples. You can also turn cold herrings into a light lunch dish by scattering them, roughly chopped, over a warm potato and beetroot salad with a **yoghurt** and mustard dressing. Or try a herring and apple salad made from marinated salted herrings: *Cut 2 filleted salt herrings into small pieces and marinate for 30 minutes in 3 tablespoons of olive oil and 1 tablespoon vinegar. In a bowl combine 4 large sliced cold cooked potatoes, 4 tart apples diced, 2 chopped hard-boiled eggs, 4 tablespoons sliced black olives, 1 small finely chopped onion, and a dill pickle finely chopped. Add the herrings. Just before serving, pour over 5 or 6 tablespoons plain* **vinaigrette** *dressing. Sprinkle with black pepper and toss well.*

Horse Mackerel   O   120 chinchard/round

This is also known as scad, and considered in the UK to be

a very poor relation of the true mackerel. But horse mackerel is quite popular in Spain and Portugal, where it often appears in the cold spiced fish dish **Escabeche**.

Horseradish

The cylindrical white root of fresh horseradish has a strong, sharp flavour. Grated, it can add piquancy to plain poached fish, but be careful to grate from the outside of the root, avoiding the centre which is the hot part. Horseradish sauce, the bottled kind, is a perfect partner for strong smoked fish like smoked eel.

Hollandaise

A hot sauce made of egg yolks and butter, rather like a warm mayonnaise, that is a rich (and therefore high calorie) but delicious accompaniment to plain grilled or poached fish. It needs to be made very carefully either in a double boiler or in a bowl over hot water, or the eggs will curdle. See **sauces**.

Huss   175 roussette/round, oily

Another name for catfish, **dogfish**, rock salmon.

John Dory

$\boxed{\text{L}}$ 100 St Pierre/flat

A very fashionable fish, despite its exceptionally ugly appearance, the john dory has a flat plump body and an enormous head, topped with a profusion of long spiny quills – always nine in number. Its thick protruding lips are permanently down-turned giving it a most lugubrious expression, as though it was about to cry. Immediately behind the oversized head is a circular black splodge, like an inky thumbprint. Continental legend had it that it is the thumb-print of Saint Peter, who threw it back into the Sea of Galilee on hearing its piteous groan.

The john dory has an exceedingly delicate white flesh that is frequently favourably compared with turbot and dover sole. It can be used as a substitute for either, and generally favours a lightly flavoured **sauce**, though the French have an interesting recipe using cloves, coriander seeds, vermouth and Pernod; where the whole fish, including the ugly head, is baked in a covered ovenproof dish. You may want to use several small john dory instead of one large one as the small ones are considerably cheaper, though admittedly a little more work will then be involved: *Thor-*

oughly clean a 2–2½ lb (800 g–1 kilo) john dory, cut off the gills and wipe it dry before rubbing it with olive oil, seasoning it well and placing it in a baking dish which has been generously brushed with olive oil. Dot the fish with small pieces of butter – about 1 oz (25 g). Then pour over the fish a mixture of 2 cloves, 6 crushed coriander seeds, 4 tablespoons vermouth, and 2 teaspoons Pernod. Cook according to the **Canadian Theory**, *basting frequently with olive oil.*

John Dory

John dory also tastes good cold, particularly in a pretty salad dressed with something fruity, like a raspberry vinaigrette: *As a starter, cut 8 oz (200 g) john dory into 12 strips and poach for 1 minute in 1½ pints (9 dl) fish stock. Turn off the heat and allow the fish to cool in the stock. When cool, remove the fish and reduce the stock by ⅔ to make approximately ½ pint (3 dl). Add 2 oz (50 g) fresh raspberries, 3 tablespoons raspberry vinegar (you can make your own by soaking raspberries in good wine vinegar for 3–4 days), and 5 tablespoons sesame oil. Boil for about 3 minutes. Cool, blend well, and pass through a fine sieve. Season with salt and freshly ground black pepper to taste. Marinate john dory fillets in the cold vinaigrette for 5 minutes while preparing a mixture of salad leaves on indi-*

vidual plates. Place fillets in the centre of each plate and spoon over the vinaigrette.

When buying john dory, remember that you will lose almost half the fish when you cut off the head. Your fishmonger should be able to tell you how much you should buy.

Julienne

Julienne is a French culinary term which means coarsely or finely shredded food, but more recently it has come to indicate fine matchstick-like strips of vegetables. Fish will frequently be presented either under, over or beside a julienne of vegetables, e.g. steamed **brill** on a julienne of vegetables is a thin white fillet of brill sitting on fine strips of carrots and courgettes arranged in a pretty criss-cross pattern.

Kebab

A perfect way to grill or barbeque fish and seafood. The French call it a **brochette**.

Kedgeree

HC

This breakfast or Sunday brunch treat combines smoked haddock poached gently in milk and then skinned and flaked, mixed in with a few chopped spring onions softened in butter to which has been added cooked long-grain rice ($\frac{1}{2}$ lb rice to a pound of haddock) and 3 or 4 hard-boiled eggs. It is based on a Hindu spiced rice dish called Khickri – but the Hindis never added haddock.

Kelt

A salmon that has spawned. A 'mended kelt' is one that has made it safely back to the sea. A lot leaner than a salmon on its way upstream, and not so tasty.

Keta

$\boxed{O}$ 360 roe

Reddish-orange salmon roe, sometimes called salmon caviar with a delicate, salty taste (nothing like sturgeons' eggs, though) and very pretty as a decoration for special fish dishes. On their own, serve them on **blinis** with fresh dill and sour cream.

Kingfish

$\boxed{O}$ 200 thazard

A type of large **mackerel**. Unrelated to the North American kingfish.

Kipper

$\boxed{O}$ 230 hareng fumé/smoked, round

Kippers are herrings that have been split, lightly-brined and then smoke-cured over wood chips. Not a breakfast dish for weight watchers, but bursting with Omega 3 for those who are heart-conscious. The healthiest way to have your kippers is in a Kipper Fillet Salad: *For 4 people you need: 8 kipper fillets, skinned and sliced into thin diagonal strips; and 1 large onion, sliced into thin rings. Place the onion rings on top of the fish and pour over 2 tablespoons of fresh lemon juice. Leave this to marinate for 2–3 hours in the refrigerator, moistening the kippers and onions with the juice several times. Drain off the juice and pour over 4 tablespoons of good quality olive oil. Sprinkle with a few fresh onion rings and fresh black pepper. Serve with brown bread and butter.*

Kokoda

Pronounced kokonda. A Polynesian marinated fish dish often served as a starter in the better resorts of Fiji and Tahiti, where they bill it as Poisson Cru au Lait de Coco. In

Tahiti they make it with tuna, but any firm fleshed fish will do – even cod, as long as it is fresh: *Dice 1 lb (400 g) fresh fish into chunks 1 inch by ½ inch and place in a plastic or china bowl. Squeeze the juice of 4 limes on to fish and leave for at least 10 minutes. Then, strain off the excess juice and add ½ chopped onion or 3 chopped spring onions, 1 grated carrot, 1 chopped tomato, and 1 tablespoon of seeded diced cucumber. Season to taste and pour on ¼ pint (3 dl) of* **coconut** *milk. Chill and serve, garnished with coriander or chives.*

Kulibiaka

See Coulibiac.

Lamprey ☐ 220 lamproie/round

This looks rather like an eel, only uglier. The most primitive of all living vertebrates, lamprey lives the life of a vampire in both fresh and saltwater. Regarded as a delicacy in Bordeaux, where it is stewed in claret and in Portugal where it is cooked with brandy and port. Treat as **eel**.

Leek 36

The leek, once the humble staple of soups, stews and stocks is fast becoming a designer vegetable. One multi-starred French chef describes leeks as 'poor man's asparagus', and they are indeed appearing on both sides of the channel in dishes such as a starter of scallops on a bed of leeks cut into thin strips, poached in water and a little butter. Across the Atlantic, grilled salmon appears on an identical julienne of leeks, sautéed gently in butter. Leeks also star in Poor Man's Asparagus Salad with Prawns: *Blanch bisected leeks for 10 minutes in boiling water before coating them with a good vinaigrette, chives and hard-boiled eggs and tossing them with cold cooked prawns.*

It is important to clean leeks well: the easiest way is to cut the green leaves away, split them down the middle lengthways, and soak them in cold water for about 10 minutes before cooking. Leeks are easy to overcook – they are best steamed, or poached very gently in ½ oz (12 g) of butter and 2 tablespoons of water, turning every few minutes for a maximum of 10 minutes.

Lemon

This is the indispensible aid for fish cooks. If all you have is a lemon, a fish and a little butter, you can squeeze some of the lemon on the fish before you bake it or grill it and with the rest of the juice and some of the zest make lemon butter to serve with the fish. Julienne the rest of the peel and scatter the thin strips over the fish as a garnish. You can use the zest in a lemon **sauce** for grilled white fish: *Make a roux by melting 1 oz (25 g) of butter in a pan and stirring in 1 oz (25 g) flour. Cook for 2 minutes, then gradually stir in ½ pint (3 dl) fish* **fumet** *or bottled clam juice. Add the juice and zest of 2 lemons, and allow to simmer very gently for about 5 minutes. Meanwhile, beat egg yolks in a bowl, and little by little, stirring continually, add about a quarter of the hot sauce to the egg yolks. Stir thoroughly then return the egg mixture to the sauce. Allow to thicken, without boiling, season with salt and black pepper. Serve fillets or grilled fish steaks placed in a pool of the sauce, garnished with a sprinkling of lemon zest.* 1 tablespoon of lemon juice has no calories – 1 fl oz (25 ml) of flesh and zest has 4 calories.

Lemon-grass

A dried herb, looking unimpressively like dried grass stalks, but most impressive once it is cooked. Lemon-grass gives

fish an exquisitely delicate, highly exotic, lemon perfume –
wonderful when cooked en papillote with fillets of lean
white fish like lemon sole. It should be used sparingly –
about one stalk crumbled, per papillote. Unfortunately, it
seems to be available only at Asian and Chinese provision
stores.

Lemon Sole $\boxed{\text{L}}$ 100 sole limande/flat

A cousin of the dab and the plaice, and can be used as such.
Small ones, if fresh, should be plain grilled, sprinkled with
parsely and served with a slice of savoury **butter** – lemon is
ideal. They can also be baked on the bone in **foil**, with
courgettes and white wine: *Clean and remove the upper skin
of small lemon soles (one per person) and place each one in
a large piece of foil. Rub the fish all over with a cut garlic
clove, sprinkle with lemon juice and cover with thinly sliced
courgettes. Season very well, and pour over 1 tablespoon of
wine to moisten courgettes. Dot with small pieces of butter
½ oz (12 g), seal the foil and bake. See* **foil.** Larger lemon
soles should be filleted (as flat fish) and used as **plaice** fillets.
If you can get hold of lemon-grass, try lemon sole fillets,
seasoned, dabbed with a little butter, moistened with a little
white wine and wrapped in a foil envelope with a strand or
two of lemon-grass. Bake according to thickness of fillets à
la **Canadian Theory** (plus 5 minutes for the foil) and open
at the table to share the exotic aroma.

Lettuce   12

In fish cookery, lettuce has a much wider use than merely as
salad or as a base for a prawn cocktail. It makes a very
pretty **coulis**, and also appears in a number of dishes as a
'wrap' – making little packets for oysters or scallops, parcels

for sea bass or salmon fillets, or a complete envelope for a salmon and rice **coulibiac**. In all these instances the lettuce needs to be blanched in boiling water for 5 minutes, rinsed in very cold water, and drained before the leaves are removed. *Wash the large leaves from 2 lettuces (you will need 3 or 4 leaves for each person). Blanch in boiling water for 60 seconds, dip quickly into cold water, then drain. Remove the hard central rib from each leaf. Season 4 fish fillets (salmon or sea bass are ideal, but you could try something humbler, like trout) and wrap them in the lettuce using 3 or 4 leaves per fillet. Lightly butter a baking dish and sprinkle with 1 oz (25 g) of finely chopped shallots. Lay the lettuce parcels on top of the shallots and pour over ½ pint (3 dl) fish stock, and 6 fl oz (175 ml) dry white wine. Cover with foil, and place baking dish over a high heat, until liquid is just 'trembling' – about to boil. Move dish to oven and cook for 10 minutes at 400 °F/200 °C/Gas Mark 6. Remove the dish from the oven and carefully lift out the lettuce parcels, using a slotted spoon. Set them aside, keeping them warm. Return stock to a high heat, reduce by boiling until syrupy, add 3 tablespoons single cream and return to the boil. Just before serving, remove the sauce from the heat and stir in 2 oz (50 g) butter in tiny pieces, whisking well to melt it, to give sauce a special sheen. Pour sauce in a pool on each plate and place a lettuce parcel in the centre.* Not for dieters, given all the cream and butter.

Lime

The good news for fish lovers is that limes are becoming increasingly available, not just in city supermarkets, but in tiny village greengrocers as well – and at not much more than the price of a lemon. Just try squeezing lime on your fish fillets next time instead of lemon and see what a difference it makes. Fresh lime, a little fresh grated ginger root and a sprinkling of fresh chervil or coriander, or even parsley, if that is all you have, baked in foil can turn a rather dull fish fillet or steak into a sophisticated supper. Even the humble sardine becomes a designer dish when marinated in fresh lime juice, grilled and served with a yoghurt, **cucumber** and lime sauce. But the easiest way to preserve limes, if they only come your way occasionally, is to make up cylindrical rolls of lime **butter** and keep them in the freezer, wrapped in foil. If you want to make a little lime go a long way, pop the whole lime into boiling water for 30 seconds before squeezing it – you will get a lot more juice from it.

Ling   L   84 lingue/round

The largest of the cod cousins, the ling can frequently weigh well over 100 lbs. Treat as **cod**.

Livers

While most fish livers are discarded along with the rest of the innards during cleaning, the red mullet liver should always be kept: it is part of the red mullet's unique flavour. The monkfish liver also has a flavour all its own. In France you can occasionally find marinated monkfish livers, but on this side of the Channel no one at Billingsgate has yet been able to track down a supplier. Given the number of monkfish served in UK restaurants every week, there must be an awful lot of livers somewhere.

Lobster   L   110 homard/crustacean

Live lobsters are not scarlet, as one might expect, but navy-blue. They turn bright red on boiling. Expensive – and only worth it if you know they are very, very fresh. The one saving grace in relation to their cost is that lobsters are so filling you don't need a very large portion. Just serve with a little good mayonnaise and a salad. One surprising flavour that works well with lobster is vanilla: medaillons of cold steamed lobsters served on a crisp salad of green beans and mixed leaves with a light vanilla sauce. See **monkfish**. Raw lobster served **Carpaccio** style with olive oil and lemon is delectable. If you are treating yourself to a whole lobster, you may need to know how to attack it: see diagram and instructions opposite.

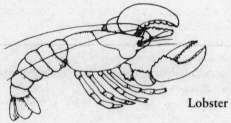

Lobster

Lox   200 +

Lox is cured salmon, usually soaked to remove excess saltiness. In the US it is traditionally served with cream cheese on a bagel.

Lumpfish   O 190 lompe/round

An ugly inedible fish, also called the lumpsucker, which has one claim to fame: its eggs or roe which are used to make imitation caviar. It tastes nothing like the real thing but is a useful decoration, only it is important to remember that it is dyed with cuttlefish ink, so always add it at the last minute or it will lose its colour and turn everything around it an inky purple.

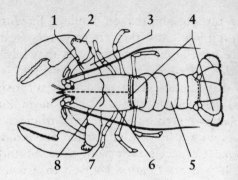

How to eat a lobster:

1 Twist off claws where they join the body, then break off small pincer and discard. Use your fingers.

2 Break claw in two at dotted line and crack with nutcracker. Dip in butter or a squeeze of lemon juice.

3 Dig out meat with small fork or use your fingers or get some help from the nutcracker.

4 Twist off tail at dotted line, then twist off flippers and discard.

5 Remove meat from tail. Hold the big end and push your fork in about $\frac{1}{3}$ of the way down; then pull. The meat should come out in one large piece. Otherwise, simply push it through from the small end to the large end.

6 Unhinge the back shell from the body. The liver is in the back and is considered a great delicacy, but not everyone likes it.

7 Remove small claws and bite off each end; there is meat inside that may be sucked out.

8 Crack the remaining part of the body along dotted line and remove meat with small fork.

Mackerel

Found in both the Atlantic and the Mediterranean, the mackerel is a handsome blue-green fish that, like the cod, suffers from its ubiquity. Fresh mackerel steaks charcoal-grilled and **blackened** with a sprinkling of Creole spices are quite delicious in their simplicity. *To make the spicy topping: Mix together 1 tablespoon paprika, 1 teaspoon cayenne pepper, ½ teaspoon white pepper, ½ teaspoon black pepper, 1 teaspoon garlic powder, 1 teaspoon onion powder, ½ teaspoon crushed dried oregano, and ½ teaspoon crushed dried thyme. Brush fish steaks with a little olive oil then sprinkle the spicy seasoning mix all over, making sure the fish is coated. Place the fish on a grill rack and cook on both sides till well blackened on outside and cooked through.*

An equally simple but delicious dish is a whole mackerel poached in white wine and vinegar and served cold with salad the next day – Maquereau au Vinaigre et Vin Blanc: *Clean and gut 4 small mackerel, running them under cold water to ensure they are absolutely clean. Crush 1 clove of garlic, slice 1 onion and 1 carrot into rings and add them*

*with 1 stick of chopped celery, 1 bouquet garni and 1 clove
to 1 pint of boiling water. Simmer for 15 minutes. Add 4
tablespoons white wine vinegar, and 4 tablespoons white
wine, 6 black peppercorns and a level tablespoon of sea salt
and bring back to the boil. Place the mackerel side by side
in a shallow dish. Slice a lemon in fine circles and arrange
this on top of the mackerel. Pour the boiling liquid over the
fish, sprinkle with sprigs of parsley and allow to sit for at
least 12 hours before serving.*

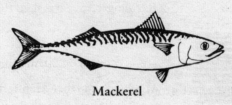

Mackerel

Mackerel works as well with cider as with wine: *Season 4
mackerel fillets with lemon, salt and pepper and place them
in a lightly oiled baking dish. Cover the fish with 2 finely
sliced apples and 2 small finely sliced onions. Sprinkle with
1 crushed bay leaf, add 1 small clove and pour over ¼ pint
(1.5 dl) cider. Cover and bake at 425 °F/220 °C/Gas Mark 7,
according to thickness (see* **Canadian Theory***).* Mackerel can
also be plain grilled, like a herring, and served with mustard
sauce, or even more traditionally, a purée of **gooseberries**.
Like the herring, mackerel is full of Omega 3.

Mako

L   108 lean, round

This large, fast-moving and dangerous shark is sometimes
passed off by less than honest fishmongers and restaurateurs
as swordfish. You can tell the difference in the fish shop by
the skin – Mako shark has skin as rough as sandpaper, while
swordfish is smooth. In a restaurant you can tell by the

flesh -if it has white whorls it is swordfish if it doesn't it could well be mako. Treat as **shark**.

Mange-tout   64

Also known as the snow-pea, the mange-tout is an extremely attractive, but alas rather expensive, vegetable, that looks extremely effective set against white fish. It tastes, and looks, good in a salad of cold shelled prawns and mange-tout dressed with an orange **vinaigrette** garnished with small orange segments.

Mango   68

A deliciously sweet tropical fruit, now widely available in the UK, that is sometimes used to accompany crab, prawn or lobster salads, as a **coulis**, in a vinaigrette or as a garnish in a fan-shaped spread of thinly sliced segments.

Marinara

A tomato, garlic and onion sauce of Italian origin that is often combined with prawns, mussels or small shellfish to serve with pasta: *In a pan, soften 1 finely chopped onion and 2 cloves of garlic in 2 tablespoons olive oil, add 1 lb (400 g) of peeled, seeded and chopped well-ripened tomatoes, salt, black pepper, 2 teaspoons brown sugar, a good pinch each of basil, oregano and majoram and simmer for 15 minutes. Add a generous glass of white wine and the cooked chopped shellfish. Season, pour over pasta and sprinkle with lots of chopped parsley. This quantity should be sufficient for 4 servings. As a guideline, allow 5–6 oz (125–150 g) pasta per person as a main course.*

Marinate

To soak fish in a liquid (a marinade) either to moisten and
soften it, prior to grilling or barbequing, or to 'cook' raw
fish by the action of the acid in the marinade. Marinating
raw fish involves the action of lime or lemon juice combined
with olive oil and flavoured with a herb or spice on the raw
fish flesh – sea **bass, salmon, trout, tuna,** all marinate well.
Ceviche and **Kokoda** are examples of marinating raw fish.
How long you let the fish marinate is a question of how
'cooked' you want it and how thickly it is cut. The minimum
is about 10 minutes and most raw fish should require no
more than 30 minutes.

*Steaks of fish like swordfish and tuna, which would
otherwise be rather dry, usually benefit from being immersed
for at least 30 minutes in a marinade of ¼ pint (1.5 dl) olive
oil, a small chopped onion, a garlic clove, a bay leaf and
perhaps a little thyme or herb of your choice, a squeeze of
lemon juice, and salt and pepper. The marinade can then be
used to baste the fish during cooking. Brochettes of cod are
much improved by marinating.*

Mariniere

A method of cooking **mussels** or other shellfish, which
involves immersing the shellfish in a large closed pot, in
which onion, garlic, parsley and white wine have been
simmered, and leaving them to steam open in the heat of the
liquid.

Marjoram

Use sweet marjoram sparingly in soups, stews and some
stuffings.

Marlin   [O]   138 marlin/round

A cousin of the swordfish rather than the shark, marlin is
not an Atlantic native, but is increasingly imported here
from warmer waters. Smoked marlin is quite delicious, if
you ever see it on offer. Treat as **swordfish**.

Marmite

A large earthenware pot usually with a lid. A petite marmite
can now be used for any clear savoury soup or type of stew
cooked and served in an earthenware pot. The traditional
Parisian marmite was of meat and vegetables but, increasingly, you find marmites of fish on restaurant menus.

Matelote

A fish stew made with white or red wine (or in Normandy
with cider), in which a variety of freshwater fish is cooked,
and almost always some eel and bream. Like its saltwater
cousins, **Bouillabaisse** and **Bourride,** a Matelote is usually
served with pieces of bread – untoasted in some regions,
toasted in others, and in some it is cut into heart shapes and
fried: *In the Loire, a Matelote is made with white wine –
they use 1 bottle for a 6 serving pot – in which is simmered
for 15–20 minutes 3–4 lbs (1.5 kilos) of various fresh fish
(perch, carp, roach) and eel (the eel being much improved if
it is marinated several hours beforehand in 3 tablespoons
brandy and 3 tablespoons oil), a large chopped onion, 2
crushed garlic cloves, the white of a chopped leek, a bouquet
garni, 1 teaspoon salt. Remove the fish and keep warm.
Thicken the stew liquid with a* **beurre manié** *made from a
heaped tablespoon of flour and 2 tablespoons butter mixed
together and divided into little balls, which are stirred gradu-*

ally into the stew. Meanwhile simmer a dozen or so tiny button mushrooms and baby onions in a little butter till tender. Place in a large soup tureen with the fish and the eel, pour over sauce and garnish with bread and chopped parsley.

Mayonnaise   HC

Mayonnaise is the most useful of sauces, either on its own or as a base for herbs and other flavourings. But at 120 calories a tablespoon it is not included in many diet sheets. If you are watching your weight, experiment with the branded low-calorie versions – one or two are quite acceptable – and thin them down with a little yoghurt or fromage blanc, and a little white wine. Mayonnaise can be made by hand or in a blender: *Mix together 1 large egg yolk, 1 teaspoon Dijon mustard, 1 tablespoon white wine vinegar or fresh lemon juice, a pinch of salt and a little white pepper. Mix well with a whisk. Add ½ pint (3 dl) olive oil or sunflower oil very slowly – a few drops at first then in a thin steady stream, beating well all the while. Taste, and if necessary, add a little more fresh lemon juice.*

Here are some hints on mayonnaise-making:

1 Make sure all the ingredients are at room temperature – not straight from fridge.
2 Do not use farm-fresh eggs: they should be at least 2 days old.
3 Make sure the bowl is dry before you break the eggs.
4 If it curdles, try adding a tablespoon of boiling water. If that fails, try adding a little mustard, *very* slowly.
5 Keep mayonnaise covered in a cool place – but preferably not in the refrigerator.

You can use your imagination with mayonnaise variations, but here are some suggestions:

Antiboise: *using 1 tablespoon each of chervil, parsley, coriander and a little garlic.*

Avocado mayonnaise: *with 1 puréed avocado, 1 teaspoon of lemon juice and a dash of tabasco – good with crab or scallops.*

Cucumber mayonnaise: *with 2 tablespoons chopped cucumber and a pinch of dill.*

Green mayonnaise: *add 1 tablespoon each of spinach, watercress, chervil, parsley, tarragon and chives.*

Mustard and dill mayonnaise: *add 1 tablespoon each of mustard and dill.*

Orange Mayonnaise: *using the rind of 1 orange and adding orange juice instead of lemon juice at the end of the recipe.*

Red pepper and Anchovy: *with 1 puréed, grilled and peeled red pepper and 1 anchovy fillet – or two according to taste.*

Medaillons

Term used for fish which has been cut into the small round or oval shapes.

Megrim   100 cardine/lean, flat

Also called whiff and sail-fluke, the megrim is another deepwater flat fish with St Peter's thumbprints, which lacks the delicacy of its smarter cousins (the turbot, the brill and the halibut), but has slightly more flavour than its other cousin, the flounder. It can be rather dry, so cook it with plenty of liquid. Treat as **plaice** or **lemon sole**.

Meunière

Method of cooking fish in which it is seasoned with salt and pepper, lightly coated with flour and then pan-fried in butter.

Microwave

Most fish and shellfish can be cooked in a microwave, but require much less time and a little less liquid than if you were using traditional cooking methods. The Massachusetts Division of Marine Fisheries, which has extensively re-searched fish cooking methods, suggests reducing the liquid by a quarter and the cooking time by three quarters. How-ever, the time factor does vary from microwave to mic-rowave, depending on the power supply, so it is wise to consult the manufacturer's cooking guide and to experiment with inexpensive fish before consigning a whole salmon or turbot to your microwave.

Positioning the fish within the microwave is important, as there is always more heat at the outside of the dish. Place fish with their thin ends pointing to the centre of the dish and the thicker ends towards the outside. Tails of whole fish cook much more quickly than the rest of the fish so it is a good idea to wrap a small piece of tinfoil around tails to stop them from overcooking. Whole round fish should be diagonally slashed at intervals to allow heat to escape, or the skin might burst.

Fish fillets and steaks are usually better cooked covered, either with a lid or plastic wrap which has been pierced to allow steam to escape. Whole fish can be cooked uncovered, but should be well seasoned with salt, pepper and lemon juice. When adding herbs, spices and seasonings, be generous – microwave cookery seems to require more flavouring than traditional cookery methods. A simple, quick microwave dish: *Place 2 hake steaks in a shallow dish, sprinkle with lemon juice, salt, pepper, 4 tablespoons of white wine, and 2 teaspoons chopped dill, dot with half a teaspoon of butter, cover and cook for 4 minutes.*

Mint   12

If you don't have any basil and the recipe requires it, try substituting mint. It won't taste the same, of course, but it will provide a surprisingly tasty alternative, especially for fish like red mullet which need a full-flavoured herb. In New Zealand, where everyone grows mint to use with all that lamb, mint is often used with trout. Springs of mint are placed inside the trout before baking, and a slice of mint butter and a sprig of fresh mint are placed on top before serving. Barbequed trout is sometimes stuffed with chopped mint and sprinkled with a mixture of mint and brown sugar before grilling.

In California, mint appears mixed with tomato and lime juice in a vinaigrette to pour over grilled tuna that has been marinated for 30 minutes in olive oil and chopped mint. A similar vinaigrette is also served with a salad of warm grilled scallops: *Simply mix 2 finely chopped shallots with 2 chopped tomatoes, 1 tablespoon of lime juice, 2 tablespoons chopped mint, 4 tablespoons olive oil.*

Monkfish   98 lotte/round

Also known as angler-fish, monkfish is rarely ever sold with its head still attached, for the simple reason it is quite exceptionally ugly and would put potential purchasers right off! The delicate white flesh has been compared to both lobster and scampi and it is said that some unscrupulous

restaurateurs try to pass crumbed monkfish off as scampi –
though given the cost of monkfish these days, it would
probably not make much of a difference to the profits!

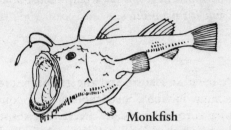

Monkfish

The real reason chefs feature monkfish on their menus so
frequently is its versatility; it is equally well-suited to
poaching, steaming, baking, grilling, and even plain *roasting*
with a dozen whole cloves of garlic, which lose their bitterness during the roasting process and turn quite sweet.
Though monkfish can be cut into cubes and grilled on
skewers, poached as steaks or steamed as fillets, it is
probably most attractive when it is kept in one piece. Ask
for a tail piece and try baking it with baby onions: *Clean
and trim a 2½ lb (1 kilo) monkfish tail, sprinkle it well with
the juice of 1 lemon, and season with salt, black pepper and
a dash of cayenne pepper, and lay it in an ovenproof dish.
Peel 1 lb (400 g) baby onions, heat them gently in 1 tablespoon of half oil and half butter until it turns golden.
Remove with a slotted spoon and pour the butter and oil
mixture over the fish. Add onions, 1 bay leaf, ½ teaspoon
thyme and 1 glass of white wine. Cover and bake at
425 °F/220 °C/Gas Mark 7, basting occasionally.*

Monkfish is also delicious poached or steamed and then
served cold, especially as a substitute for lobster on a salad
with a vanilla bean sauce. To make the sauce: *Heat 2 oz
(50 g) chopped shallots and a vanilla bean in ½ pint (3 dl)*

*white wine and ¼ pint (1.5 dl) white wine vinegar and
reduce to 3 tablespoons. Strain, then into the strained liquid,
very gradually, add 3 oz (75 g) of butter. Place small chunks
of monkfish on a salad of very lightly cooked green beans
and mixed leaves and pour the sauce over the fish.*

Mornay

Fish dishes served à la mornay are generally covered in a
white **sauce** to which has been added equal quantities of
grated Gruyère and Parmesan cheese. It is often lightly
browned under a hot grill immediately before serving.
Smoked fish in a white wine or cider sauce lends itself admirably to the Mornay treatment.

Mouclade   HC

A version of **mussels** marinière, where the sauce is thickened with cream and egg yolks or cornflour, and flavoured
with a pinch of curry or saffron.

Mousse   HC

A mixture of cold cooked fish, egg whites, cream and seasoning. Given the cream content of most mousses, dieters
should avoid them on restaurant menus, but if you are
making your own, you can substitute half the cream for a
mixture of yoghurt (or low-fat fromage frais) and skimmed
milk; or use a mix of ⅔ cows' yoghurt (or fromage blanc)
and ⅓ skimmed enriched milk. For a simple, easy to
prepare fish mousse recipe, take: *1 lb (400 g) cooked fish (if
you have some salmon or pink trout, try mixing pink and
white fish together), finely chopped and beaten together with
salt, pepper, ½ teaspoon chopped dill and 3 tablespoons of*

single cream and yoghurt mixed. Add 2 stiffly beaten egg whites. Pour mixture into a buttered ovenproof dish, which is sitting in a shallow baking dish of hot water or **Bain Marie**. *Bake at 360 °F/180 °C/Gas Mark 4 for 20 minutes. Allow to cool, unmould carefully and decorate with fresh dill, and serve with* **watercress** *sauce.* For a 2 or 3 layer mousse, mix the pink and white fish in separate bowls, then pour them into the cooking dish in layers. But be careful – you will need to allow each layer to chill slightly, before pouring in the next – or the colours will run.

Mousseline

Quite often used to describe a **mousse** made lighter and richer by the addition of extra, often double, cream. It can also describe a sauce that has been enriched by the addition of whipped cream.

Mushroom   16

Mushrooms are most often used in fish cooking either as a stuffing for whole fish or as part of a base or 'bed' of herbs and vegetables on which fish is placed to be steamed, braised or cooked en papillote. *To prepare the mushrooms for either stuffing or as a base: Heat a tiny amount (1 teaspoon should do) of butter or oil in a pan, add 1 small finely chopped onion then a cup of washed, chopped mushrooms, including the stalks. Heat very gently till softened, add a teaspoon of chopped parsley and remove from the heat to mix with fresh breadcrumbs for stuffing or herbs and other vegetables for a* **duxelle***, or 'bed'.* Trout stuffed with mushrooms, parsley and lime juice garnished with thin slices of lime and very thinly sliced raw mushrooms is a simple but effective dish.

Mussel

L̲ 90 moules/shellfish

Full of zinc and iron as well as Omega 3, the mussel is another underrated little fellow who is exceptionally versatile, and very good value. Mussels can be eaten raw from the shell, but you really need to know just where your mussels have come from. It is generally wiser, unless you have picked them yourself off a beach that you can guarantee is unpolluted, to eat your mussels cooked.

One of the simplest ways is to grill them on the half-shell: *First, beard the mussels, then wash them very thoroughly and steam for 5 minutes in ½ inch boiling water to open, discarding any that do not open. Remove the empty upper shell and sprinkle the lower half-shell with a few breadcrumbs. Brush these with a tiny amount of garlic butter and place under a very hot grill till brown. Sprinkle with fresh chopped parsley and serve hot.*

The most traditional way to serve mussels is Moules Marinière: *Add 2 quarts of well-scrubbed and bearded mussels to a pot in which has been heated ½ pint (3 dl) white wine (or ¼ pint (1.5 dl) wine and ¼ pint (1.5 dl) vermouth), 2 oz (50 g) of butter, 4 tablespoons finely chopped spring onions or small onions, ½ a crumbled bay leaf, ¼ teaspoon thyme and 2 sprigs of parsley. Close the pot tightly, place over a high heat and boil quickly for 5 minutes, shaking the pot regularly so that all the mussels are exposed to the heat at the bottom. Within 5 minutes all the shells should be open. Remove the mussels with a slotted spoon into large soup bowls or one large serving dish, sprinkle with at least 4 tablespoons of chopped parsley and serve with fresh French bread.*

A more glamorous use of mussels is with sake and coriander. In the original recipe the mussels were combined with roasted oysters, but they are just as good on their own:

Sauté 1 thinly sliced onion and ½ stick of celery, chopped, in 1 oz (25 g) butter. Add 1½ oz (37.5 g) chopped fresh coriander, 1 tablespoon of chopped chives, ¾ oz (20 g) chopped fresh ginger, 2¼ lbs (900 g) freshly scrubbed and bearded mussels, 1 pint (6 dl) sake and 1½ pints (9 dl) fish stock. Cook over high heat until the mussels have opened, then remove them. Reduce liquid slightly to thicken, add 2 tablespoons lemon juice, adjust the seasoning, and pour over the mussels which have been arranged in a large serving bowl. Garnish with sprigs of coriander.

Mustard

Given that mustard is traditionally associated with beef and sausages, it is surprising that it goes so well with fish. A few simple diagonal slashes in a mackerel, herring or sardine filled with a mustard and butter mix and placed under a hot grill transforms an inexpensive fish into a tasty supper dish: *Try 3 teaspoons of mustard to 1 teaspoon of butter, season with fresh ground black pepper, salt and lemon juice, and sprinkle with chopped dill or parsley before serving.* And mustard and dill sauce is the best possible companion for **gravad lax**, or **gravad mac**; *to 1½ pint (3 dl) of mayonnaise, either home-made or low-cal, add 2 tablespoons mustard and 1 tablespoon chopped dill.*

Tarragon also teams well with mustard, either in a tarragon and mustard mayonnaise or a mustard and tarragon butter. Should you have any fresh eel steaks: *Mix ¼ cup mustard, with 2 tablespoons white wine and 1 tablespoon of olive oil. Marinate eel steaks in this mixture for 1 hour before grilling. Baste with the marinade mixture during grilling.*

Nantua

A fish dish described as Nantua or à la Nantua is usually decorated with crayfish or served with a crayfish sauce or both. Poached sole is sometimes presented this way.

Niçoise

À la Niçoise means, in culinary-speech, with tomatoes and garlic, but to most people it indicates a salad of tuna, anchovies, potatoes, green peppers, green beans, sliced onion rings, olives, quartered hard-boiled eggs and tomatoes in a garlic vinaigrette dressing, which must be made with olive oil. Traditionally, Salade Niçoise is served without lettuce as a starter, but mixed in with crisp lettuce leaves and a really good vinaigrette it makes an attractive summer lunch dish out of not much more than a can of tuna, a tin of anchovies, a dozen olives and a few cold potatoes. But good olive oil is essential for the vinaigrette: *Line a salad bowl with the leaves of 1 large lettuce. In a separate bowl, mix 4 sliced cold cooked potatoes, 4 ripe tomatoes, 6 black olives and 6 green olives (or 12 black), 1 small thinly sliced onion,*

2 sticks of sliced celery, 2 chopped hard-boiled eggs and a tin of flaked tuna fish. Pour over a dressing made from 2 tablespoons of lemon juice, 5 tablespoons of olive oil, 1 tablespoon of finely chopped anchovy fillets, and 2 table-spoons finely-chopped parsley and toss well. Pour into the salad bowl and garnish with anchovy fillets sliced length-wise.

Octopus |L| 78 poulpe/cephalopod

Like the abalone, the octopus needs to be beaten with a
wooden mallet (or even a heavy stone, if that's all there is to
hand) before it is tender enough to eat. It is said to need
'ninety-nine bashings' before it's ready. The Octopus looks a
fairly fearsome adversary to prepare when you first get hold
of him. What you should do first is cut the head off above
the tentacles, turn the head inside out, discard all the innards, remove the eyes and the mouth, wash it thoroughly
in running water for at least 5 minutes, and then start
pounding. A slightly more cowardly way for those who don't
fancy turning the head inside out, is simply to use the tentacles and throw the head away at the start.

Octopus can be eaten raw in a **Sashimi** dish, or charcoal-
grilled with lemon and butter, but it is probably most
palatable when braised gently in red wine with plenty of
garlic and then served either hot, or cold on a leafy salad:
Cut the tentacles, or body and tentacles into bite-size pieces.
Blanch for 1 minute in boiling water, remove, and then
simmer gently in well-salted water for 30 minutes. Wipe the
meat dry, then brown it lightly in 2 tablespoons olive oil in

which you have softened 1 chopped onion and 2 cloves of garlic. Add ½ pint (3 dl) red wine and ½ pint (3 dl) water, a **bouquet garni***, 1 teaspoon oregano, and 2 tablespoons chopped parsley. Cover the pan and simmer gently till soft, about 1 hour. Sprinkle liberally with parsley before serving – hot or cold.* Octopus is also an interesting addition to brochettes: Try it (after it has been blanched and simmered) lightly brushed with oil, well-seasoned, then grilled on a skewer with onion and green pepper and served with fresh tomato sauce.

Oil   `HC`

To make a good vinaigrette or a good mayonnaise you need good oil. Rather buy a small bottle of really good olive oil than scrimp on a big bottle of something inferior. The best you can get is extra virgin olive oil from the first pressing, but virgin olive oil from subsequent pressings is almost as good. Olive oil, being mono-unsaturated is now regarded as being best for your health – though not necessarily your waistline. However, some people do find that mayonnaise made from olive oil is a little over-flavoured. If it is too strong for your personal taste use safflower, peanut or sunflower oil. Dieters should note that 1 teaspoon of oil (5 ml) is 40 calories. The nut oils – such as hazelnut and walnut – have the same calorie value.

Olive

Olives, especially black ones, add a touch of Mediterranean or Ionian sunshine to the humblest of fish dishes, whether they are chopped up in a stuffing for grey mullet, crushed into softened butter for black olive butter to serve with marinated and grilled swordfish steaks, blended with anchovies to make **Tapenade,** or olive and anchovy **butter,** baked in white wine with **whiting,** mixed and softened with fennel, onions and garlic to fill and decorate a red mullet or red snapper, or simply scattered over a fish salad. Before using stoned olives, blanch in boiling water for 3 minutes then drain in cold water to remove the pickling brine or oil. Olives, incidentally, are only 3 calories each.

Omelette

The most famous fish omelette is probably the Omelette Arnold Bennet, created in 1937 by the Savoy Hotel's then chef de cuisine, Jean Baptiste Virlogeux, for Mr Bennet who was a regular late-night diner. It's still on the menu and much favoured for post-theatre suppers. The Savoy's instructions are: *Beat 3 eggs, add a soup spoon of gruyère cheese chopped into ¼ inch cubes, salt and pepper, then add 2 soup spoons smoked haddock cut into ¼ inch cubes and a little more black pepper. Beat with a fork, then pour into an omelette pan. When nearly cooked, but still fluid, pour over sufficient* **sauce** *mornay to cover, sprinkle with grated parmesan cheese and brown quickly under a very hot grill.* Most smoked fish, lightly flaked, makes a tasty filling for an ordinary omelette – especially smoked salmon, which should be cut into small pieces and scattered over the omelette just before folding. A 2-egg omelette, sprinkled with 2 oz (50 g) of smoked haddock, and made in a non-stick pan lightly brushed with oil (no more than ½ teaspoon) will work out at about 230 calories.

Onion   28

Onions are most useful vegetables, whether you are using ordinary onions, shallots (the tiny purple French onions) or spring onions (the long salad ones). Essential for soups, stews and marinades and a great added flavour when incorporated into a **duxelle** with mushrooms or vegetables underneath baked fish, or a stuffing for whole fish. In fish cooking, onions usually need to be softened either in butter (you only need a teaspoon) or in a little fish stock. If you don't like your onions to be too oniony, blanch then first in boiling water for 3 minutes.

The French have an onion sauce they serve with inexpensive fish like haddock and hake, called Sauce Soubise which uses: *1 lb (400 g) of onions simmered in 1 oz (25 g) of butter. Add this to a ½ pint (3 dl) of béchamel* **sauce** *to which ½ glass of white wine or fish stock has been added, plus salt, pepper and a little nutmeg. Purée in blender or push through a sieve and reheat gently before using.*

Orange   60 approx per fruit

Oranges go surprisingly well with cold crustaceans – especially prawns, when used in an orange **vinaigrette** or in *a warm orange butter sauce: Heat the juice of 1 orange in a stainless steel pan with 1 oz (25 g) of butter. Boil quickly for 20 seconds. Then remove pan from heat and whisk in a further 1 oz (25 g) of butter cut into small pieces. Pour over cooked and cooled prawns and serve.* Shellfish also work well with oranges – there is a recipe dating back to 1747 which stews scallops in white wine and orange juice. And salmon with blood orange sauce is now appearing on menus from London to LA – a very nouvelle combination of pink and orangey-red. Dilute orange with a little lime if you find it too sweet.

Orange Roughy   L 140

Deep sea perch with orangey-red scales and an exceptionally

white flesh which is noted for both its delicacy and its versatility. Caught off the New Zealand coast and marketed throughout Australasia and the US, Orange Roughy is one of the few fish that tastes almost as good after freezing as fresh. Use it in any recipe for the equally versatile **monkfish**.

Ormer

Another name for **Abalone**.

Oyster   ♡ L 56 huitres/shellfish

More people would eat oysters if they knew how full of vitamins and minerals they are (Casanova used to eat fifty a night to improve his stamina) and how low in calories: less than seventy-five calories per half dozen oysters. And the good news is that now they are being more widely culti-vated, the price of oysters is, in real terms, falling.

There are several kinds of oysters available in the UK; the most common of these, and generally the most highly regarded, being the Native, the round brownish-shelled *ostrea edulis*, which is grown in Kent, Essex and Cornwall – these are the colchesters, whitstables and pyefleets. Also available in the UK is the Portuguese oyster, the *crassostrea angulata*, which is usually slightly larger than the edulis, with a beige or white coloured shell. These are the oysters grown in French oyster basins (claires) and known as fines de claires. Becoming more popular in the UK, and gaining increasing respect from oyster cognoscenti is the Pacific or Japanese cupped oyster, the *crassostrea gigas*, which is now being farmed extensively on the west coast of Scotland, where the purity of the deep water lochs is proving perfect for breeding. Oysters are at their best with lemon juice, a little black pepper, sea salt and some very fresh brown bread, but they can be grilled (*very* quickly: 5–10 seconds) on the half-shell, threaded on a skewer, or poached *briefly* in fish stock, shallots and white wine or champagne. To open oysters see **shucking**.

Paella

Named after the two-handled frying pan in which the rice base is served, Paella traditionally contains not just seafood, but chicken, vegetables, pork and garlic sausage. However, there is no reason why you can't create a purely seafood paella: *Cod, whiting or hake is ideal as a base fish plus prawns, shrimps, and mussels, along with onion and garlic, tomatoes, red peppers, kidney beans, fish stock and a pinch of saffron. Heat 2 finely chopped onions, 2 crushed cloves garlic and 1 large red pepper, de-seeded and sliced, in 2 tablespoons oil. Add 2 large peeled, seeded and chopped tomatoes, and stir in 1 lb (400 g) of rice. Cook over a low heat for 5 minutes. Then cover with fish stock or bottled clam juice (available in most good delicatessens) together with a pinch of saffron. Add 4 oz (100 g) of peas and 4 oz (100 g) of kidney beans (already prepared) and cook for a further 10 minutes before adding 1 lb (400 g) of white fish cut into bite-sized pieces, ½ lb (200 g) of prawns or shrimps and two cups of well-washed mussels. Turn heat up and boil for 5 minutes, before lowering heat to simmer for a further 15 minutes, adding further stock if necessary to get a moist but not mushy or over-liquid consistency.*

Pan-frying

Pan-frying is shallow-frying as opposed to deep-frying. Very little oil or clarified butter is needed – just enough to cover the bottom of the pan. Fish to be pan-fried should be lightly dusted with flour. See also **Frying**.

Papillote

En papillote is the French term for cooking in parchment or **foil**.

Paprika

Dried and ground sweet red pepper. Used more as a garnish than a flavouring in most fish cookery, though it is often added to Eastern European fish soups and stews to give a sweet and spicy warmth – like Hungary's **carp** soup.

Parrot Fish $\boxed{L}$ 86   cacatois

A brilliant blue and yellow fish which looks as though it has escaped from an aquarium. Parrot fish are flown in fresh (on beds of ice) from the Seychelles and available in some more adventurous fishmongers. Small ones can be grilled to maintain their exotic colouring, larger ones should be treated like sea **bream**.

Parsley   24

A most underrated herb. Chopped fresh parsley as a garnish will liven up the plainest of fish dishes, but don't chop the leaves too finely, or too neatly. If you have no other herb in the house except parsley, use it to make a parsley **butter** to serve atop grilled fish, plus a whole sprig of parsley as garnish. Parsley is an important ingredient in **green sauce** and complements most other herbs. It's also very good for you: high in Vitamin C, carotene and organic salts and a very effective antidote to an overdose of garlic. It really does get rid of the smell.

Pasta

The increasing popularity of pasta means it is appearing more frequently as an accompaniment to seafood dishes, though more often with shellfish than fish. Both scallops and mussels look, and taste, good with pasta. Tinned **clams** are the main ingredient of the time-honoured Vongole Sauce, which can be made with red or white wine. For the white wine vongole sauce: *Heat 2 minced cloves of garlic in ¼ cup of olive oil, add a half cup of clam juice or the juice from the tinned clams, 2 tablespoons white wine, a generous pinch of salt, fresh black pepper, 1 tablespoon of chopped parsley and a 10 oz (250 g) tin of clams, very finely chopped. Serve on top of 1 lb (400 g) of thin pasta cooked al dente (still slightly firm to touch) and sprinkled with parsley.*

For fish sauces the thin stranded pastas: linguine, taglierini and spaghetti and the very thin 'angel hair' are better than the broader tagliatelles. A recent arrival on the pasta scene is black linguine or angel hair, which is made from ordinary pasta dough to which has been added the ink from the ink sac of a large **cuttlefish**.

Pastis

Anise-flavoured liqueur. See **Anise**.

Paupiette

Thin fillets of fish (**plaice** and lemon sole are ideal) covered with some kind of filling or **stuffing**, rolled up and then cooked slowly in a fish fumet or in white wine. The cooking liquid can then be reduced and made into a sauce to serve with the paupiettes.

Pepper

Red peppers, green peppers (which are young red peppers) and yellow peppers (which are a slightly different family) all go well with strong fish, especially in salads. One of the tastiest uses of red peppers is when they are roasted, peeled, chilled and served with an anchovy vinaigrette, garnished with anchovy fillets – a simple but effective summer starter. Roast peppers (red, green and yellow, if you can get them) on all sides under the grill until the skins are blistered. Pop them into a sealed plastic bag for 10 minutes. When removed, they will be easy to peel and seed. Rinse, dry and cut them into long ½ inch wide strips. Arrange peppers on a small flat plate, pour an anchovy vinaigrette over them and decorate with anchovy fillets.

Perch | O | perche/round

A colourful freshwater fish with greeny-gold scalloped scales found in ponds, lakes and slow-moving rivers. The perch is not often available commercially, so you will need to know a friendly angler if you want to sample its very tasty flesh. If you do get a perch take care when skinning and scaling it – the spines can be rather fierce. A brief dip into boiling water should aid the scaling process. Small perch can be cooked à **la meunière** – in butter; larger ones can be stuffed and baked with plenty of white wine to keep the flesh moist.

Very fresh perch can also be used in the Flemish version of a freshwater **Bouillabaisse** – Waterzootje or Waterzooi, a simple water-based stew: *Clean 3 lbs (1 kilo 200 g) of freshwater fish and slice it into chunks (use perch, barbel, carp, eel or tench) and place this in a well-buttered saucepan together with 1 leek, 1 stick of celery, a large bunch of parsley stalks, a bouquet garni and salt and pepper. Cover with water and cook briskly for 20 minutes so that the liquid reduces as the fish are cooking. Add fried croûtons, and serve sprinkled with freshly chopped parsley.*

Peri-peri

Sometimes called piri-piri. A hot chillie-based sauce often used as a dip for crustaceans and shellfish in Africa, the West Indies, and Asia. You will need to buy peri-peri oil from an Asian delicatessen, or you can make your own: *Soak 2 small fresh chillie peppers in a ¼ pint (1.5 dl) of olive oil in a screwtop jar for 3 or 4 days. Blend together ½ lb (200 g) ripe peeled tomatoes, 4 oz (100 g) chopped onions, 2 oz (50 g) chillies, 1 oz (25 g) chopped garlic and braise gently in 2 tablespoons of peri-peri oil till soft – about 30 minutes. Add 2 crushed bay leaves, a little salt to taste and stir well. Cool and sieve or blend again briefly before serving as a dip.*

Pickling

Pickled fish is fish that has been cured in salt and vinegar and then pickled in a solution of vinegar, sugar, salt and spices. Herring is the most popular fish for pickling but almost any fresh fish can be pickled. *To cure fish: Place in a glass, ceramic or plastic jar with a solution of 12 oz (300 g)* salt to 2 pints water (1.1 litres) and 2 pints (1.1 litres) white vinegar (do not use either wine or cider vinegar). Make sure the fish is covered by the liquid, close the jar firmly and refrigerate for 3–7 days, depending on the size. Once cured, rinse the fish well, and place it in the following pickling liquid: 2 pints (1.1 litre) white vinegar, 1 pint (6 dl) water, 3 tablespoons sugar, 1 tablespoon salt, 1 sliced onion, 1 garlic clove, 1 teaspoon each mustard seed, peppercorns, bayleaf and cloves in a refrigerated air-tight jar for approximately 1 week.

Pie

A fish pie can be an inexpensive family dish when made with whiting, coley or cod and a light cheesy sauce with a potato topping; or a more glamorous and more costly supper dish when filled with a variety of fish and shellfish, in a sauce flavoured with wine and parmesan cheese, and topped with a rich golden pastry. The following recipe is a basic one, which can be fancified by adding cooked shrimps, prawns, mussels or even scallops: *Poach 1½ lbs (600 g) mixed fillets of fish very gently for 10 minutes in ½ pint (300 ml) of milk, with 2 crumbled bay leaves. Set aside to cool and prepare a potato topping by mashing 1 lb (400 g) boiled potatoes with 1 oz (25 g) butter and a little hot milk. Hard boil 2 eggs, and peel and slice them. Flake fish into a buttered pie dish, making sure you extract all the bones and any skin. Add the sliced hard-boiled eggs and a table-spoonful of chopped tarragon (parsley will do, if you haven't any tarragon). Make a* **roux** *with 1 oz (25 g) butter and 1 oz (25 g) flour and cook for 2 minutes, then add the milk which the fish was poached in. Stir well and add a pinch of dried mustard and 1 oz (25 g) of parmesan cheese. Season to taste and add to fish. Allow to settle for a few minutes, then* *spread the potato mixture over the top and bake for 15–20 minutes, until the top is browning.*

Pike

L 100 brochet/round

A long slender freshwater fish with a very large mouth and very strong teeth. Its firm white flesh is much more esteemed in France than in the UK, where it is most often found on menus as **quenelles** de brochet – creamy dumplings of pike,

Pike

which should be avoided by those watching their weight. In the Loire region of France, where pike is usually commercially available (here many restaurateurs catch their own), it is most frequently poached in a **court-bouillon** and served with a simple **beurre blanc**.

Pilchard

O 260 sardine/round

A pilchard is an adult **sardine**.

Plaice

L 86 plie/flat

One of the smaller members of the flat-fish family, you can tell when a plaice is really fresh because its spots are a very bright orange. As it gets older the spots get progressively duller. A small fresh plaice needs nothing more than a very hot grill and a slice of lemon. One factor is critical with plaice, however you cook it: it must *never* be overdone or it will lose its delicate taste. If you are unsure about your oven temperature, undercook it rather than overcook it.

Larger plaice are better filleted, and the fillets poached or baked **en papillote** with a dab of butter, a little white wine and some citrus juice: Try lime or half lemon and orange together with plenty of fresh chopped parsley. *Plaice can be very prettily presented as* **paupiettes***: Fillet the plaice, following* **flat fish filleting** *instructions, so that you have 4 long thin fillets (or buy 4 plaice fillets), season well and lay flat, making sure that the fleshy side that was against the central bone is now on the outside. Gently sweat ½ lb (200 g) spinach in 1 oz (25 g) butter till soft then make a purée. Do the same with ¼ lb (100 g) sliced mushrooms and mix the two together. Season with salt, black pepper and a dash of nutmeg. With a knife, spread the mixture thickly along the upper side of each plaice fillet, season with salt, pepper and lemon juice and roll up, starting with the thickest end and rolling it towards the narrowest. Secure with a toothpick and place the paupiettes in a small ovenproof dish so that they are nestled side by side. Pour 1 glass of dry white wine, or a mixture of wine and fish stock, over the paupiettes, cover with foil and cook in moderate oven 400 °F/205 °C/Gas Mark 6, according to the* **Canadian Theory***. If the fillets, plus fillings, are 1 inch thick, cook for 10 minutes, plus an extra 5 minutes for the foil cover. When cooked, remove the fish, reduce the liquid and thicken it with a little* **beurre manié** *or a spoonful of cream or creamy yoghurt, and garnish with watercress sprigs.*

Poaching

Poaching is cooking fish in simmering, not boiling liquid, which can either be water, wine and water, milk, a **court-bouillon**, or a fish **stock**. One of the problems about fish poaching is extracting the fish from the poaching liquid without breaking it. If you don't feel a fish poacher is worth the investment, make your own by fitting a wire cake rack into a deep baking dish that will sit on top of your hob. Or you could, with a large whole fish, wrap it in cheese-cloth or a clean tea-towel (or even a stocking or the leg of a pair of tights), tie the ends and drape each end over the poaching dish, lifting the cloth and enclosed fish out when cooked. Small fish or steaks can usually be managed with a slotted fish slice. Very thin soft-textured fish fillets are not usually suited to poaching as they tend to break up in poaching liquid. Thicker fillets, steaks and small fish should be placed in a poaching liquid which is already simmering; large fish should be placed into cool liquid which is brought to a simmer. Make sure the fish is covered with liquid.

Because of the very few added calories, poaching is an ideal fish treatment for slimmers.

Pochouse

A Burgundian version of the **Matelote**, Pochouse is a kind of freshwater bouillabaisse generally featuring carp, pike, bream, burbot and plenty of eel, simmered in white Burgundy and thickened with a **Beurre Manié**: *Cut 1½–2 lb (600–800 g) freshwater fish into pieces and place in a large pan on a bed made of 1 large thinly sliced carrot, 1 large sliced onion and 1 clove of garlic, chopped. Season well, add a large* **bouquet garni** *and cover with dry white wine (perhaps an inexpensive Vin de Pays from the south-west, if you want to save the Burgundy). Bring to the boil, cover and simmer for 20 minutes. Remove the fish from the liquid and place it in a second pan in which you have already sautéed 2 oz (50 g) chopped bacon and 4 oz (100 g) sliced mushrooms and 8 oz (200 g) baby onions together in a little* *oil. Thicken the liquid with pieces of* **beurre manié,** *using 2 oz (50 g) butter mixed with 3 oz (75 g) flour. Strain, then pour over fish and serve with garlic* **croûtons.**

Pollack   84 lieu jaune/lean, round

Another relation of the cod, this fish is distinguishable by its yellowish sides. Treat as **cod** or **haddock** and use in any of those recipes which suggest taking 'a pound of white fish'.

Pomfret   L   brème de mer/round

In America, pomfret is another name for butterfish, a type of bream; but in the UK it is also used to describe small flat white fish with swallow-like fins, and a quite deliciously delicate very white flesh. These are flown in from the Indian Ocean and generally, though not always, sold frozen. If you can get fresh, then simply grill them and serve with lemon and fresh chopped parsley. If frozen, thaw and bake in foil with lemon juice, a few small dabs of butter and lots of fresh chopped parsley.

Potato   100

Everyone knows that fish goes well with deep-fried potatoes, whether you call them frites, French fries, or just plain chips. Much healthier – and prettier – are tiny boiled new potatoes, liberally sprinkled with fresh parsley or fresh chives. Warm potato salad made from potatoes that are boiled, peeled, chopped and tossed in **vinaigrette** while still warm makes an appetising base for marinated herrings or flaked smoked fish and chopped hard-boiled egg with lots of fresh chopped parsley. They are also featured in **Salade Niçoise** and in **Herring** and Apple Salad.

Mashed potatoes can be used in **salmon cakes** or **smoked fish** gratinée – if you use hot milk to mash potatoes you will have less trouble with lumps. Baked potatoes can provide a light fishy lunch if filled with a half and half mixture of sour cream and fromage blanc and topped with flaked smoked fish, sprinkled with parsley. Or even better, mix the fromage frais and sour cream with small pieces of smoked salmon. For a luxury baked potato, use sour cream topped with keta, the pretty pink salmon caviar.

Poutargue

See **Botargo.**

Prawn   L   120 crevette/crustacean

There are two kinds of prawns generally available in the UK: the large northern or deep sea prawns, mostly cooked as soon as they are caught off Greenland, and frozen for importing to the UK – these are red both before and after boiling; and the common prawn, from shallower British, French and Mediterranean waters, which is colourless and turns pink on boiling. Most prawns are cooked as soon as they are caught because they keep so badly, but if you buy fresh prawns they are delicious grilled with a little garlic **butter** and served plain or with a spicy dip such as the **peri-peri** sauce. Alternatively, try threading them on to skewers to grill either on their own or with other fish and shellfish.

Prawns can be bought ready-peeled but it is much cheaper to peel your own:

1 Hold prawn in left hand and break off its head with right hand.
2 Grip the legs on one side of the body at the end near

the head and pull off the legs and the shell attached.

3 Pull off remaining shell except for tail, which is useful to hold on to when you dip your prawn in sauce.

If you want to 'butterfly' prawns before you grill them, you will need to devein them. Make a narrow deep cut right along the centre back of the peeled prawn, but making sure you do not cut right through. Extract the dark vein with the point of a knife, then spread the prawn flat. Wash and dry before seasoning and brushing lightly with a little oil or garlic **butter**. Try sprinkling butterflied prawns with dried fennel seeds before grilling.

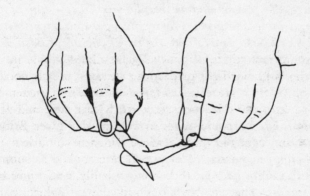

How to butterfly prawns:

Peel the prawn, leaving just the tail on, then cut along the back of the prawn, but not all the way through. Spread it open in a butterfly shape.

Peeled prawns make attractive salads and starters: a circle of chilled prawns on a warm potato and basil purée with a champagne **vinaigrette** is fairly simple to execute but looks and tastes stunning: *Peel and devein 16 large prawns. Poach*

*the prawns in a fish stock for 3 minutes, turn off the heat
and allow them to cool in the stock. Meanwhile, boil 1 lb
(400 g) peeled and diced potatoes with ½ chopped onion
and 5 large basil leaves in enough salted water to cover the
potatoes. When the potatoes are soft, drain them well and
pass them through a coarse sieve into a clean pan. Blend
with 1 oz (25 g) butter and ¼ pint (150 cl) cream. Set aside
and prepare 4 oz (100 g) finely* **julienned** *blanched vegetables
(carrots, leeks, celeriac). Gently mix these vegetables with
the cold prawns in a vinaigrette made from 5 tablespoons
olive oil, 1 tablespoon tarragon vinegar, 1 tablespoon white
wine, salt, pepper and a ½ pint (3 dl) of champagne. Spread a
bed of the basil and potato purée on to 4 individual plates.
Arrange the prawn and vegetable mixture on top of the
purée, dribble additional vinaigrette over and garnish with
small Cos lettuce leaves and a sprig of chervil or basil.*

Also attractive for summer lunches (and very easy to
prepare) is Prawn Gazpacho: *In a processor, blend together
a 15 oz (375 g) tin peeled chopped tomatoes in their juice;
four peeled fresh tomatoes, chopped; 1 large stick of celery,
chopped; 1 red pepper, seeded and chopped; 1 green pepper,
seeded and chopped; 1 cucumber, chopped; 2 tablespoons
fresh chopped coriander leaves; 2 cloves garlic, chopped;
¼ pint (1.5 dl) tomato juice; 2 tablespoons red wine vinegar, 2
tablespoons olive oil, 2 tablespoons lime or lemon juice, 1
teaspoon of sugar, a pinch of cayenne pepper and a dash of
tabasco sauce. Chill. If the mixture is too thick, thin with a
little chilled fish stock or bottled clam juice. Just before
serving stir in 1 lb (400 g) roughly chopped peeled prawns
reserving 4. Decorate with the remaining 4 whole peeled
prawns. This quantity serves 4 people as a main course lunch
dish.*

Provençale

Provençale generally indicates the inclusion of some or all of the following: tomatoes, olives, basil, onions, parsley, capers, gherkins, garlic and olive oil. Provençal sauce is a simple but effective way of spicing up plain grilled fish. Kebabs of white fish, even of cod, can look quite glamorous if the white fish cubes are alternated on the skewer with green peppers and served in a pool of rich red provençale sauce, scattered with a few chopped fresh basil leaves. *The simplest provençale sauce is made by cooking: 3 chopped cloves of garlic, 1 large chopped onion, and 1 lb (400 g) of peeled and seeded chopped tomatoes (or a tin of peeled tomatoes, drained and chopped) over a gentle heat for 20 minutes, then adding 1 heaped tablespoon each of chopped basil and chopped parsley, 1 tablespoon of tomato purée, 2 tablespoons red or white wine and, if you have it, ½ small chopped sun-dried tomato. Simmer until the sauce is thick. Just before serving, sprinkle in 3 or 4 chopped black olives.*

Purée

A fish purée is prepared by mashing, sieving or blending in a mixer cooked fish, or shellfish. This can then be mixed with a sauce or stock to gain the desired consistency. For a simple shrimp or prawn purée, which could be used to garnish plain poached or grilled fish: *Finely grind ¼ pint (1.5 dl) cooked but unshelled shrimps or prawns, mix together with an equal quantity of thick **béchamel** sauce. Heat gently and then strain through a sieve before serving, underneath or poured over plain poached fish. Garnish with whole peeled shrimps or prawns.*

Quahog

A species of **clam**, most commonly found on the US Atlantic coast, that is regarded as the best clam for making **chowder**.

Quenelle $\boxed{\text{HC}}$

A kind of oval dumpling made from finely ground fish; the word is apparently a French adaptation of the Anglo-Saxon word knyll, meaning to pound or grind. The most common quenelles on restaurant menus are of pike (brochet). They are often difficult to make successfully at home (impossible if you don't own a blender), but here is a fairly straight-forward recipe (very rich and not for the calorie-conscious), that can be made with most white fish: *Blend 1 lb (400 g) of white fish fillets with 5 eggs whites in an electric mixer till the fish is finely ground. Add 1 pint (6 dl) of thickly whipped cream to the fish and make sure all the ingredients are well blended together. Add salt and pepper and chill for 3 hours. Prepare a sauce (crayfish is the recommended one, but, given the shortage of those, a prawn or shrimp sauce would be an appropriate substitute) and vegetables of your choice. 10 minutes before you want to eat, have a large, shallow pan of lightly salted water ready simmering, but not boiling. This is the tricky bit: take 2 tablespoons and warm them in boiling water, scoop out a mound of the fish mixture in one spoon, using the other spoon to make a smooth egg-shape. Then carefully slip it into the barely simmering water. Dip spoons in boiling water again and repeat the process, working quickly until the pan is full or you have used up your quenelle mixture. They should need about 8 minutes each – but test a little earlier to see that insides are still creamy. Remove them as they cook – in the order you put them in – with a slotted spoon and serve with the sauce and vegetables.*

Quiche

Smoked fish, smoked salmon, prawns and shrimps are all appropriate toppings for a quiche. For a simple (but rich and calorific) prawn quiche: *Mix 1 cup of milk with ¼ pint (1.5 dl) double cream and 4 egg yolks, ½ teaspoon salt, fresh ground black pepper, and a good pinch of nutmeg, stir well till thick. Take your already prepared pastry shell, and cover the base with 1 lb (400 g) of finely grated gruyere cheese mixed with 1 tablespoon of grated parmesan cheese. On top of this place ¾ lb (300 g) cooked and peeled prawns, pour in the egg mixture and bake for approx 25 minutes at 400° F/200°C/Gas Mark 6.*

For a lower calorie quiche, try smoked fish in yoghurt on a wholewheat base. *To make pastry: Rub 3 oz (75 g) diced butter into 6 oz (150 g) wholewheat flour until the mixture resembles fine breadcrumbs. Stir in 6 teaspoons cold water and mix to form a pastry dough. Turn out with floured hands on to a lightly floured board, and roll out so that it is large enough to cover the base and sides of an 8 inch*

(20 cm) quiche dish. Prick the pastry base with a fork and bake 'blind', using foil or pastry marbles to keep base flat, in a pre-heated oven at 400° F/205° C/Gas Mark 6 for 10 minutes or until golden.

Meanwhile, remove any skin and bones from 6 oz (150 g) cooked and flaked smoked fish. Cover the base of the cooked pastry case with flaked fish and sprinkle with 1 tablespoon of chopped parsley. Beat together 3 eggs and ¼ pint (1.5 dl) plain yoghurt, and season with plenty of black pepper and just a little salt, as the smoked fish is already quite salty. Pour this egg mixture over the fish, sprinkle with 1 tablespoon grated Parmesan cheese and return to oven. Bake at the same temperature for 20–25 minutes. Sprinkle with a little more fresh chopped parsley and serve hot or cold.

Raw Fish LC

Fish that is eaten absolutely raw in the Japanese fashion is usually **Sashimi** or **Sushi**. Raw fish that is lightly treated with oil and lime or lemon is usually presented as either **Carpaccio** or **Tartare**. Fish that is uncooked but marinated in lemon or lime so that it loses its rawness, and looks and tastes as though it has been lightly cooked can be found in a **Ceviche** or **Kokoda**. Raw fish is perfect for slimmers – there are no added calories.

Ray

See **skate**.

Redfish   112 rascasse/lean, round

Also called Ocean Perch, the redfish is a distinctive bright orangey-red in colour with a rich creamy-brown flesh that turns white and flaky when cooked. In Eastern Europe it is usually stuffed and baked in a similar manner to sea **bream,** or used in a cold fish soup. In Marseille they consider their redfish, the rascasse, an essential ingredient for a true **Bouillabaisse**.

Red Mullet   ☐O☐ 160 rouget/round

If any fish epitomizes the taste of the south of France, it is the red mullet – especially when it is stuffed with fennel and olives or mounds of fresh basil. During the summer months they are caught in British waters, and these colder water specimens are considered superior in taste to their Mediterranean cousins. Take advantage of their freshness then and grill them: *Cut off the gills, but leave the heads on and do not gut. Wash and dry, make several slashes on each side. Brush well with olive oil, pop a little fresh chopped basil in each slash, season with lemon juice, salt and pepper and grill. Serve with a slice of basil butter*. Be warned though – small red mullet can be rather bony.

During the winter you can use frozen red mullet to make a **Soupe de Poisson**.

Red Snapper   ☐L☐ 116 vivaneau/round

An attractive semi-tropical fish that has begun to make regular appearances at Billingsgate, mostly frozen but increasingly available fresh, by way of the Seychelles. A fish with firm, white flesh with quite a strong, distinctive flavour. Because of this, and the fact that most red snapper in the UK have been frozen, they are best filled with a well-flavoured **stuffing** (fennel, anchovy and olive would work) or baked with a fairly strong sauce like a **Provençale**, using extra red peppers. Snapper heads are large in proportion to the body – you could lose up to 45 per cent – so make sure you buy sufficient weight. Cold fillets of snapper, poached, cooled and cut into fingers, served red side up in a **walnut** vinaigrette around a nest of salad leaves makes a light, attractive starter. A more glamorous version of this has the red snapper served warm in the shape of a butterfly: *Buy enough red snapper fillets (or red mullet) to make 16 pieces. Sauté fillets quickly in hot olive oil, skin side first, until crisp. Form a butterfly 'body' on each plate with a small mound of radiccio and slim strips of carrot and courgette, with chive strings for the antennae. Arrange 4 warm red snapper fillets on each plate, to resemble wings. Warm ¼ pint (1.5 dl) fish stock in pan. When hot, add 3 tablespoons walnut oil, and 1½ oz (approximately 40 g) butter, stirring till well-blended, then pour over red snapper to serve warm.*

Reduction

The method of reducing the volume of a liquid by boiling to give it a thicker consistency and a more intense flavour. Fish **stock** can be reduced by boiling to make a fish **fumet** which can be used as a base for fish sauces.

Red Wine

Forget that old story about only white wine with fish. In Bordeaux where they know a thing or two about wine – and food – they not only drink chilled claret with fish right through the summer, they cook with it too. Freshwater fish from the Gironde, and saltwater fish from the Atlantic coast are cooked à la Bordelaise, braised in red wine. They even do their salmon in red wine, braised slowly and served with tiny onions and mushrooms. Salmon in red wine was a popular dish on this side of the Channel too, back in the 18th century, and a version of that recipe is still served – with the salmon being poached in red wine, which is then reduced to make a sauce. It is also served in California with a red wine **butter** called variously Cabernet Butter, Pinot Noir Butter or Zinfandel Butter, after different Californian red wines.

Rémoulade

This is a mayonnaise-based **sauce** flavoured with capers, grated onion, garlic, parsley, tarragon and chives, lemon juice and a dash of anchovy essence, which can be served with cold shellfish.

Rhubarb   8

Puréed rhubarb makes an attractive pink tart sauce to accompany oily fish like mackerel: *Peel rhubarb, cover with water, add just a little sugar and boil till soft. Sieve or blend to a purée. If it tastes too sharp, add a little more sugar or a dash of orange juice.*

Risotto   HC

A seafood risotto is an easy and attractive supper dish, but not one that can be prepared in advance. It should take about 20 minutes and should be served immediately: *Sauté 3 chopped baby squid, 4 whole large Pacific prawns, 6 small peeled prawns and a dozen or so mussels in a little olive oil for 2 minutes, then remove the seafood from the oil. Add ¾ lb (600 g) rice. Let it absorb oil for 3 minutes then add 1 pint (600 cl) of fish stock and a glass of white wine. Stir well and continue to cook, adding more fish stock when necessary, for about 15 minutes, and until rice is tender but not mushy – al dente, as the Italians would say. Just before serving add a little fresh chopped basil, stir once and serve.*

Roach $\boxed{O}$ 140 gardon/round

Freshwater fish of the carp family, with delicate, but very bony flesh. Most often dipped in milk, then flour and shallow-fried, but it can be used in **carp** recipes.

Roasting

Large pieces of fish can be roasted in the oven just like a joint of meat; the heat sears the outside and forms a crust to contain the juices inside. Fish has much less fat than meat so it needs to have its outside surface well moistened with butter or oil before roasting, and should be basted regularly throughout cooking. It needn't be covered. Monkfish is a good roasting fish – providing you have a large thick tail section – especially when cooked with garlic: *Rub the cleaned fish all over with garlic, sprinkle liberally with lemon juice, salt and black pepper, then brush generously with melted butter or good oil. Surround the fish with lots of large whole blanched and peeled garlic cloves – allow at least 3 per person. They lose all their bitterness during cooking and taste quite sweet. Serve the fish with the pan juices and the garlic.*

Rock Salmon

See **dogfish**.

Roe $\boxed{O}$ Herring: 92/Cod: 128

These are fish eggs; the most popular being those of the cod and the herring. Soft herring roes can be sautéed in a little butter and mixed with mustard and parsley to make a tasty paste for toast. Hard cod roe is usually bought ready-cooked (if not, tie it in muslin and boil it for 20 minutes) and served heated and sliced with a tasty **sauce** such as anchovy. Cod roe can also be puréed with olive oil and garlic to make **taramasalata** (though purists would make this out of carp or mullet roe), or mixed with cream cheese to make a very easy pâté: *Simply blend 4 oz (100 g) smoked cod roe which has been skinned with 4 oz (100 g) of cream cheese, 1 small grated onion and the juice of half a lime or lemon. Decorate with stoned black olives.*

Grey mullet roe is also pressed and salted to make the continental delicacy **botargo**, sometimes called poutargue, which is served in slices rather like a salami. For sturgeon roe, salmon roe and lumpfish roe, see under **caviar, keta** and **lumpfish** respectively.

Rollmop

Whole boned herrings, made into rolls around pieces of onion and cucumber and **pickled** for 4 or 5 days in a spicy wine or cider vinegar **marinade**.

Rouille

The hot pink sauce that accompanies a traditional fish soup or a **Bouillabaisse**. There are several different methods, but the simplest is: *Mix together, ideally in a blender, ½ pint (3 dl) of mayonnaise with 4 crushed cloves of garlic, 2 small finely chopped red chillie peppers, 1 teaspoon of tomato purée and a dash of tabasco.* The Greek version of rouille is **Skorthalia**, which is thickened with bread and/or potato. Traditionally, Rouille is served in a small dish, accompanying the soupe de poisson and the croûtons. The Rouille is then spread (or dolloped) on to the croûtons before they are floated on top of, or immersed in, the soup. Grated cheese can also be served; this is sprinkled on top of the Rouille, after it has been spread on the croûtons.

Roulade

Usually a flat piece of fish that has been spread with a filling of either vegetables and herbs (spinach is excellent for this) or a purée of another fish or shellfish, rolled up, cooked (either in **foil** or poached in a **fumet**) and served in slices like a swiss roll. The following Fish and Spinach Roulade can be made with most white fish – whiting is tasty and inexpensive: *Cut 8 oz (200 g) fish into thin slices (about ¼ inch thick) and make sure there are no bones. Roll out 8 oz (200 g) of puff pastry (frozen is fine) into a thin rectangle with straight edges. Make a purée from 10 spinach leaves heated gently in a pan in 1 oz (25 g) of butter and then blended or sieved. Mix into this 4 oz (100 g) mozzarella cheese, cut into tiny pieces, and season well. Spread purée over the pastry so that it comes to within ½ inch of the edge. Lay fish on top of the puree, sprinkle with 2 table-spoons chopped parsley, and roll up carefully, so that it looks like a swiss roll. Brush top with a little melted butter, scatter with a few poppy seeds if you have them, place on a well-oiled baking tray and bake at 400° F/205° C/Gas Mark 6 for 30 minutes.*

Roux

A mixture of roughly equal quantities of butter and flour heated for approximately 5 minutes while being stirred con-stantly, which is then used as a base for many sauces in-cluding **béchamel** and **velouté**. It is also used to thicken some soups and stews.

Saffron

The dried stamens of the saffron crocus, dark orange in colour and giving sauces a distinctive yellow tinge, and a wonderful flavour to soups and stews. It isn't cheap, but it makes all the difference to a **Soupe de Poisson** or a **Bouillabaisse**.

Most shellfish, scallops in particular, work well with a creamy saffron sauce: *Simmer briefly several threads of saffron in 2 tablespoons of white wine, then set this aside to infuse. Reduce ½ pint (3 dl) fish stock by half. Strain the saffron liquid into the fish stock, season, and add 2 tablespoons cream. Reduce until thick and creamy. Sprinkle with finely chopped chives just before serving. For a less calorific version: replace the cream with yoghurt, which may need to be lightly sweetened. If you have only saffron powder, heat the wine and stock and add a generous pinch of saffron just before mixing in the cream or yoghurt.*

Sake

A spirit distilled from rice and sometimes used in Japanese

fish cookery. Sake is now appearing at points further west, most notably in an occidental dish of oysters and **mussels** roasted in sake and coriander.

Salad

Fish, crustaceans and shellfish make great salads, either well chilled or, increasingly popular, warm atop a cold bed of salad. Here are just a few suggestions:

Crab with **avocado**
Herring, Apple and Beetroot salad
John Dory and Raspberry Vinaigrette
Monkfish and Vanilla Bean Salad
Mussels in a Mustard and Yoghurt Dressing
Niçoise
Prawn and Mange-Tout in Warm Orange Butter Sauce
Octopus in Red Wine Salad
Scallop and Strawberry Salad
Skate in a Tarragon Vinaigrette
Smoked Eel with Almonds and Orange, in a Yoghurt
    Dressing
Smoked Fish and Warm Potato Salad
Squid in Sesame Seed Vinaigrette

Salmon   140–190 saumon/round

Salmon is one of those fish that not only looks impressive and tastes delicious but is good for you too because it is so rich in Omega 3. The bad news is that it can be rather high in calories, soaring from a low of 140 per 4 oz (100 g) portion in February, March and April to a high of around 190 per 4 oz (100 g) portion in July to October. It all depends on whether the salmon is on the way home after a couple of years at sea or whether it is heading downriver after the rigours of mating, when it will be a lot leaner. There is much debate about the merits of wild salmon vs. farmed salmon. Salmon connoisseurs agree that wild salmon does have a superior flavour, but most connoisseurs will add that, provided a farmed salmon is well-bred, well-prepared and well-presented, it is very hard to tell the difference. This was confirmed by a taste test run by a national newspaper, when some fish experts found it almost impossible to tell the difference. Apparently, the only way they could tell was by looking at the tails – farmed salmon tails are rounded at the edges; it gets so crowded in the cages that they keep bumping their tails against one another. Salmon farming certainly has helped to bring salmon prices down. A whole farmed salmon is now an affordable treat, and makes a stunning centrepiece for a special dinner or a summer luncheon party. Because of its high level of fish oils, salmon is rich, moist and very filling. The simpler the treatment the better.

Salmon

The easiest way to cook a whole salmon, if you are serving it hot, is to wrap it in foil: *Season it well, sprinkle it inside and out with sprigs of fresh dill, add a few tiny dabs of butter, a little white wine to moisten it, seal well and cook according to the* **Canadian Theory**. *Garnish with savoury dill* **butter**, *and lots of fresh dill sprigs*. Or you may to prefer to **poach** your salmon in a **court-bouillon**, and serve it hot with a **cucumber sauce** or cold with a green herb **may-**

onnaise. The simplest way to poach a large salmon (though not exactly the most elegant) is to put the salmon inside one leg of a pair of tights, tie a knot at each end and lift it in and out of the poaching liquid that way.

If your salmon is in steaks, you can grill it and serve it with slim circles of lime and ginger **butter** (brush the steaks with cut ginger root and sprinkle them with lime juice before grilling), or cook the steaks en papillote with chopped fresh mint, a dab of butter and a little wine to moisten. If you only have a small tailpiece of salmon, make it go further by cutting it into chunks and grilling it together with a white fish on skewers. Alternate pieces of pink and white fish, served with a light green sauce – perhaps **watercress** – looks impressive and tastes terrific.

Salmon also lends itself admirably to marinating lightly as **Tartare** or **Carpaccio**, and to pickling as **Gravad Lax**; and smoked salmon is one of the easiest and most effective first courses you can serve. Don't add chopped onions and capers the way some restaurants do, simply garnish with a slice of lemon and serve with brown bread and a black pepper grinder. Smoked salmon also makes the best sandwiches in the world, but only on very fresh brown bread.

Because salmon is so rich (and filling) you need allow 4–5 oz (100–125 g) per person with fillets, 6–7 oz (150–175 g) for steaks. Because you will lose almost a third in the head and tail, you will need a 2 lb (800 g) salmon for 4 people.

Salt

Fish can be very successfully cooked either on a bed of sea salt – **sardines** are exceptionally tasty cooked this way, and don't taste at all over-salted – or completely coated in a crust of rock salt. This method is an interesting way of totally containing the juices within. A whole grey mullet, a small bream or a small fresh red snapper could be cooked this way: *The fish should be left whole, with head and tail intact, but with gills removed and innards extracted through as small a slit as possible just below the head. Then wash the fish and dry well before placing it in a baking dish on top of a thick bed of rock salt. The entire fish should then be coated with a layer of rock salt, making sure that none of the fish is visible. It should then be baked fairly slowly at about 350° F/190° C/Gas Mark 4 for 45 minutes to an hour, depending on the size of the fish. The salt will form a strong thick crust which will need to be cracked and peeled off before serving, with an appropriate sauce – perhaps anchovy, made by adding 3 or 4 minced anchovy fillets to a ½ pint (3 dl) of* **hollandaise** *sauce.*

Those who have been advised (often because of high blood pressure) to cut back on salt need not worry about baking fish in a crust of salt. With this method all the salt is removed when the crust is broken away.

Salting

Salting is a way of preserving fish by either coating it in salt and placing it in a container with holes in the bottom to allow the moisture to escape, for several days, or immersing it in a brine solution of salt and water. Salted fish should always be well soaked in fresh water before use – up to 24 hours depending on the saltiness of the fish – and the water should be changed regularly. There have been suggestions that the abnormally high incidence of stomach cancer in some areas of Japan could be related to their exceptionally high intake of salted fish.

Samphire   8

A bright green seaside vegetable sometimes called sea
asparagus or sea fennel. Readily available on the Norfolk
coast and now being sold with increasing frequency by the
better fish merchants, it is quite delicious and deserves a far
wider market. Serve it on its own as a starter, steamed or
cooked for 5–8 minutes in fast-boiling salted water and
served with **hollandaise sauce**, just as you would fresh
asparagus. Blanched for 30 seconds in boiling water then
refreshed in very cold water it becomes a crunchy addition
to a salad. Or sauté in a little butter and serve as a vegetable
with fish dishes. As a sauce, samphire will add glamour to
the most humble of fish: *Boil ½ lb (200 g) samphire (use
only the tips, not the hard stalks) fast in salted water for
about 8 minutes, refresh in cold water. Then drain and purée
in a blender with 2 oz (50 g) of butter, a little black pepper
and a dash of lemon juice. Heat but do not boil.*

Sardine   O   225 sardine/round

An excellent source of Omega 3, calcium and the Vitamins
A and D. Fresh sardines are at their best when they are
treated simply: cleaned, gutted and plain-grilled; just
sprinkled with lemon juice or, like herrings, slashed diagonally and grilled with a dab of mustard. Or try them
grilled on a bed of sea salt, using a kind of dry-frying
technique for which you will need not only a sturdy frying-
pan but also a kitchen extractor fan, as dry-frying tends to
create a great deal of smoke: *Heat a frying-pan till very hot,
and cover the base with a thick layer of very coarse sea-salt.
Place cleaned sardines on top of the salt layer and cook over
a very high heat for 2–3 minutes on each side or till well-
crisped on the outside. No, they won't taste oversalted.*

Sardines can also be lightly grilled then marinated in olive oil and lime juice: *Gut, bone and remove heads of sardines (about 4 fish per person). Wash, dry and split open to lay them flat. Brush both sides with olive oil and grill very quickly, about 30 seconds each side, retaining the pan juices. Cool and arrange the fish in a circle on a serving platter. Crush 2 cloves of garlic in the pan juices, add a little olive oil and the juice of 1 lime and pour this over the sardines. Sprinkle with chopped parsley, cover with cling film and chill for at least 2 hours. Serve alone or with a* **cucumber** *and yoghurt sauce.*

If the only sardines you have are in tins, and you need your dose of Omega 3, do not despair. Turn them into sardine and **yoghurt** pâté: *Drain 2 tins sardines, add ¼ pint (1.5 dl) natural yoghurt, the juice of 1 lemon and a pinch of cayenne pepper. Mix them together in a blender and chill well before serving with hot brown toast triangles.*

Sashimi   LC

A traditional Japanese dish of very thinly sliced, very fresh raw fish and shellfish, usually served with soy sauce and wasabi, a green horseradish. It is important to have a variety of fish with different colours and textures – for instance, mackerel (raw mackerel is surprisingly appetising) salmon and halibut, together with scallops and prawns – but even more important is to have fish that is absolutely fresh. Chilling the fish slightly will make it easier to slice more thinly and, obviously, a sharp knife is crucial. Sashimi is different from **Sushi**, which is prepared raw fish.

Sauces

Serious weight-watchers should concentrate on sauce-free

fish dishes – grilled fish or fish cooked en papillote and served with no more than a sprinkling of fresh lime or lemon juice and garnished with fresh herbs. It is invariably the sauce that contains all the calories. However, low calorie sauces are not impossible: the simplest way is to add a little fish fumet to the pan juices created by the baking or grilling of your fish or to the reduced poaching liquid. If necessary, it can be thickened with a vegetable purée (mashed potato is ideal) instead of flour and made creamier by adding a spoonful of yoghurt instead of cream, and flavoured with the herbs or spices of your choice.

For those who are not calorie counting, most hot fish sauces are an adaption of one of the four basic French sauces for fish: béchamel, which is a white roux of butter and flour to which milk is added; velouté, a white roux of butter and flour to which fish stock is added; hollandaise, a mixture of egg yolks, butter and lemon juice; and beurre blanc, which is butter flavoured with shallots, wine and vinegar.

BÉCHAMEL

Make a **roux** *by stirring 1 oz (25 g) of butter and 1 heaped tablespoon of flour slowly over a low heat for about 2 minutes, then remove from the heat. Do not let it turn golden or brown, or you will have a blond or brown roux instead of a white roux. Meanwhile slowly heat, but do not boil, ½ pint (3 dl) of milk – ¾ pint (4½ dl) if you want a slightly thinner sauce – with ½ a small sliced onion, a sprig of parsley, a bay leaf, a pinch of thyme, a grating of nutmeg, salt and pepper. Strain the milk and add a little to the roux, stirring constantly to make a thick smooth paste. Return the pan to a moderate heat and, very gradually, add the remainder of the milk stirring briskly all the time to ensure there are no lumps. Allow the sauce to boil for 1 minute, stirring regularly; it should be thick and creamy. If it is* *lumpy, press it through a sieve, return it to a low heat and simmer for 5 minutes. If it is too thick, bring it back to a simmer and, little by little, add more milk. If you have poached your fish in milk, use that milk to make your béchamel.*

To make the béchamel richer, you can add a little butter, tiny piece by tiny piece – no more than ½ oz (12 g) in all – making sure that each piece is mixed in completely before the next piece is added; a little cream, spoonful by spoonful; or, for a very rich béchamel, add 1 large beaten egg yolk mixed with 2 tablespoons cream. If you are using egg, you will need to add the béchamel to the egg, drop by drop at first, and then in a thin stream, rather than vice versa, or the egg will scramble.

VELOUTÉ

A velouté sauce is made in exactly the same way but adding a white wine-based fish stock instead of milk to the white roux. It can be thickened and enriched in the same way as béchamel – with butter, cream or egg yolk, or with a vegetable purée. For a red wine sauce, use a brown roux and a fish stock made with red wine.

HOLLANDAISE

This hot sauce of butter and egg yoks resembles a warm mayonnaise, and is a very rich but delicious addition to any plain grilled or poached fish. It needs to be very carefully made, either in a double boiler or in a bowl over hot water, or the eggs will curdle: *Boil 3 tablespoons white wine vinegar with 1 tablespoon water and 6 crushed white peppercorns until a quarter of the liquid (approximately 1 tablespoon) remains. Strain and leave to cool in a separate bowl. When cool, stand the mixture in its bowl over a pan of simmering water and mix in 3 well-beaten egg yoks. Then, very care-*

fully, as if you were making mayonnaise, in a thin steady stream, pour in 6 oz (150 g) of warm, but not hot, melted butter, stirring all the time. Add salt and a squeeze of lemon juice to taste.

That's the traditional way of making hollandaise. There is a quicker way if you have a blender. Using the same proportions, beat the eggs in the blender, then add the reduced vinegar and water. Next, add the melted butter in a steady stream with the machine switched on at low. Before use, heat the sauce gently in a thick-bottomed pan.

You can use this hollandaise as a basis for a variety of sauces, such as herb hollandaise: add chopped chervil or tarragon, or both; cucumber hollandaise: add finely chopped blanched cucumber; blood orange hollandaise: add the juice and zest of 1 blood orange (this looks stunning with poached salmon); or make hollandaise rose: add a dash of tomato purée for a pretty pink sauce.

BEURRE BLANC

This is a rich butter sauce, traditionally served with poached freshwater fish, but it also goes very well with grilled or poached flat fish. There are several ways of making beurre blanc. One of the simplest ways is: *Mix 3 tablespoons of water with 1 tablespoon of vinegar in a saucepan. Add 2 small finely chopped shallots. Reduce the mixture by two-thirds over a medium heat and cool until warm. Then, over a low heat, add 6 oz (150 g) of firm butter, chopped into small pieces. Add the butter piece by piece, stirring quickly with a fork all the time. Don't let the mixture become too hot or the butter will go oily – it should look like thick cream. Pour over poached fish and sprinkle with parsley . . . unless you are watching your weight, when you should ask the waiter to hold the beurre blanc . . . but keep the parsley. A sprig of parsley is about 1 calorie.*

BEURRE MANIÉ
A mixture of flour and butter, kneaded together to form a paste, then divided into walnut-sized pieces, and added, piece by piece, to sauces, soups and stews at the end of the cooling time, for thickening. *Use 1 tablespoon butter to 1 tablespoon flour.*

BEURRE NOIR
Beurre Noir is a basic butter sauce with added capers and parsley. It is actually dark golden brown in colour, rather than black. *For 4 people, heat 4 tablespoons of butter in a saucepan until it starts foaming and turns golden brown. Pour this over hot fish which has been previously poached in a vinegar court-bouillon, sprinkle with chopped capers and parsley. Meanwhile, very quickly, add 1 tablespoon vinegar to the pan, heat to boiling point and pour this over the fish and the butter.* Slimmers may care to note that there are 105 calories in each level tablespoon of butter ... but only one calorie in 1 tablespoon of vinegar.

Béchamel and velouté based sauces are generally less rich than hollandaise or beurre blanc based sauces, unless you've been exceptionally heavy-handed with the cream. The following are just a few sauces that can be made from béchamel or velouté:

Anchovy: *Soften 1 clove of garlic in ½ oz (12 g) butter in a small pan. Add 5 or 6 finely chopped anchovy fillets and stir over a low heat until thoroughly mixed. Add to béchamel or velouté shortly before serving.*

Aurore: *Add 3 tablespoons fresh tomato purée or tomato paste to ½ pint (3 dl) béchamel or velouté, tasting all the time to get the right flavour. Add ½ oz (12 g) butter, piece by piece, and 1 heaped tablespoon of fresh green herbs: chervil, basil, tarragon or parsley. A little sugar might help to bring out the flavour.*

Mornay: *Add 2 oz (50 g) each of finely grated gruyère and parmesan cheese to ½ (3 dl) béchamel.*

Mussel: *Simmer 1 tablespoon finely chopped shallots in ½ oz (12 g) butter, and add with a dozen or so finely chopped mussels and their juices to ½ pint (3 dl) béchamel or velouté.*

Mustard: *Add 1 tablespoon French mustard to ½ pint (3 dl) velouté, just before serving, together with ½ oz (12 g) butter, piece by piece. Do not allow to boil.*

Parsley: *Add 1 tablespoon single cream and 1 oz (25 g) butter to ½ pint (3 dl) béchamel or velouté. Reduce slightly and add a few drops of lemon juice and 2 heaped tablespoons chopped fresh parsley.*

Pernod: *Stir in 1 tablespoon Pernod or any pastis (more or less, according to how strong a flavour you want), then add ½ oz (12 g) butter.*

Prawn: *Simmer 8 oz (200 g) cooked prawns and their shells in ¼ pint (1.5 dl) white wine until reduced by half. Strain into ½ pint (3 dl) béchamel, add 2 tablespoons of single cream mixed with enough tomato sauce to colour it pink, and lemon juice to taste.*

Tarragon: *Heat 4 tablespoons chopped tarragon in ¼ pint (1.5 dl) white wine until reduced by half, and add to ½ pint (3 dl) béchamel. Reduce, and add a few small pieces of butter, plus 2 tablespoons fresh tarragon, and serve.*

Saury

See **garfish.**

Sautéeing

Sautéeing is like shallow-frying, only even shallower and much quicker. Sauté comes from the French word to leap, so anything sautéed should leap into the frying pan and then quickly out again. The small amount of fat in the pan should be very hot – use clarified butter, or half butter and half oil to avoid the butter going brown.

Scaling

See under **cleaning**.

Scallop $\boxed{L}$ 85   coquille st jacques/shellfish

An hermaphrodite mollusc that is justly prized for its slightly sweet, creamy flesh (the nut) and its pale orange roe sac (the coral). It is also much valued by chefs for its versatility. You can do almost anything with a scallop: grill it, skewer it, poach it, steam it, bake it, serve it in a salad, or increasingly popular, present it raw, as tartare of scallops: *Remove the skirting and the roes from 16 fresh scallops, rinse in lightly salted water and dry. Chop the scallops, but not too finely, then season with a splash of hazelnut or walnut oil. Mix in 2 teaspoons chopped shallots, 4 midget gherkins cut into very fine strips, a squeeze of lemon juice, salt, black pepper and a little grated nutmeg. Serve like a steak tartare, in a small pattie shape in the centre of a plate, garnished with another 4 thinly sliced midget gherkins, and surrounded by tossed salad.*

Scallops also work well with **anise** (Pernod, Ricard or pastis), with nutty or fruity **vinaigrettes** (hazelnut or raspberry), herby sauces (especially chervil and coriander), and they have a surprising affinity to hot and spicy flavours.

The Mexicans bake them with chopped green chillies, tequila and tabasco. If you are baking scallops you could use the small frozen queen scallops, but for steaming, grilling or marinating, fresh scallops are essential.

Given their delicate creamy colour scallops look particularly attractive set against a green background – steamed and served on a bed of puréed spinach or in a pool of **watercress** sauce (perked up perhaps with 2 tablespoons Pernod), or nestling on a lettuce **coulis**. Like most shellfish, scallops need very little cooking, and are better undercooked than overdone. 4 to 5 minutes will be all that is needed in a steamer, slightly less if you are poaching. For a pretty summer salad using poached scallops, strawberries and mint: *Rinse and dry 1 lb (400 g) scallops, then poach them for 3–4 minutes in the juice of 1 lemon and a dash of black pepper. Remove from heat, drain and cool. Meanwhile trim and halve a punnet of strawberries and set aside. In a large bowl, mix together 8 oz (200 g) natural creamy yoghurt, 1 tablespoon of sour cream, 2 tablespoons chopped fresh mint, the juice of 1 orange and the juice of 1 lime or lemon, ½ teaspoon ground cloves, and a dash of black pepper. Add strawberries and scallops and chill for 2 hours. Serve with a sprig of fresh mint.*

Scampi

See **Dublin Bay Prawn**.

Sea Robin

A type of **gurnard** with fins like wings.

Sea Urchin
♡ | O | 92–360 oursin/echinoderm

This spiny marine creature resembling a small black or bottle-green hedgehog is regarded as a great delicacy in some parts of France, and in the Far East, where it is reputed to have great restorative powers, especially for the morning after. It is probably something to do with the high zinc and iron content. It can be eaten raw with a dash of lemon juice and black pepper or lightly cooked and served like a soft-boiled egg with toast 'soldiers' to dip into the soft orangey-yellow roe. Only the roe is eaten.

Seaweed

Seaweed is a traditional ingredient of Oriental cookery (see **Sushi**) but is gradually making its way into the modern occidental kitchen, especially in some shellfish dishes, such as **scallops** steamed on a bed of a seaweed. Called Nori, it is available in dried sheets in specialist food shops. There are also several native seaweeds such as the Welsh laver and the Irish caragheen. Laver is a reddish green colour which turns darker green when boiled, rather resembling puréed spinach. Nothing like bread, and most experts are at loss to explain the term 'laver bread' – though laver itself can be served, in its hot cooked form, on toast with lemon juice and black pepper; or cold, mixed into a paste, rather like a **Tapenade**, with a little olive oil, lemon, garlic and black pepper. Carragheen is a small purplish-green sea plant that is used both to thicken soups, stews, and fruit flans (because of its gelatinous properties) and as the base for a variety of Caragheen desserts. It is said, when boiled with milk, to be an excellent cure for insomnia.

Sesame

A tropical plant whose seeds (and the oil from those seeds) can be used in fish cookery. Fillets of gentle white fish like flounder or plaice can be brushed with oil, then coated with sesame seeds, baked in a hot oven and served with a fresh tomato and basil sauce. **Octopus** and **squid** taste delicious in a salad made with sesame seed oil and sprinkled with sesame seeds. Take care when using the oil though, it can be overpowering if you use too much.

Seviche

See under **Ceviche**.

Sewin

A Welsh sea-trout. See under **trout**.

Shad $\boxed{\text{O}}$ alose/round

Another fish that is more highly prized by our neighbours across the channel than it is here. Shad is a cousin of the herring, which migrates upstream to spawn, and is oft condemned in this country as having too many bones. In Bordeaux they stuff the shad with sorrel leaves, and serve with a sorrel purée, which is alleged to soften the bones. Prepare as **herring**.

Shallot

A small onion that is slightly less sharp than an ordinary onion and thus easier to digest. Usually used in preference to onions in fish sauces.

Shark   L   108 requin/round

Sharks have a surprisingly poor image in the fish business –
perhaps the movie *Jaws* destroyed its hopes of becoming a
major attraction on restaurant menus. However, things
could be looking up for afficionados of shark meat. Once
sold mainly as frozen steaks, whole fresh sharks are becoming an increasingly common sight at Billingsgate market.
Shark can be rather dry, so it is a good idea to marinate it
in oil, wine, chopped onion and herbs before grilling either
as steaks or in chunks on a kebab. Shark can also be braised
in wine like **tuna**.

Shrimp   L   134 crevette grise/crustacean

A translucent grey-brown turning brown when boiled,
shrimp can be eaten whole, but they are generally peeled.
They are a useful addition to salads, sauces and as a garnish
for grilled fish – you can make a savoury shrimp **butter**:
*Mix 2 tablespoons of mashed shrimps into 4 oz (100 g) of
softened butter. Or serve them potted – mashed in butter
with a little anchovy or essence of anchovy added.*

Shucking

Watching the oyster-openers in action out in front of those
smart Parisian brasseries, shucking an oyster looks incredibly easy – until you try it. The secret is to do it slowly,
carefully, and with either thick gloves or a heavy cloth to
protect your hands, both from the rough oyster shell and
the sharp knife. The experts do it in the palm of the hand,
but until you have had some practice it is wiser to shuck the
oyster on a bench or table top. First, rinse the oysters in
cold water. Then place an oyster flat-side up on a firm

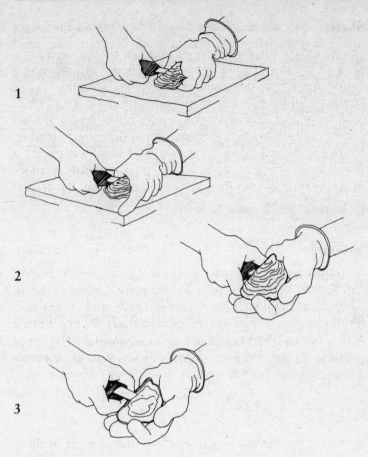

Shucking oysters:

1 Either place the oyster firmly on a board or hold it in a gloved or covered hand.
2 Insert the knife tip close to the hinge and twist it to enter. Swing the knife along the inside of the top shell to cut the muscle. Remove the top shell.
3 Loosen the meat from the shell by running the knife between the meat and the shell.

surface, with the hinge side pointing out. Hold the oyster firmly in your left hand, with a cloth between your hand and the oyster shell. Insert the tip of a very sharp knife into the hinge end, then twist the knife sharply to force the hinge open. Then run the knife along the inside of the top shell right around, so that you sever the muscle which holds the shells together. Next, loosen the meat in the bottom shell by running the knife between the shell and the oyster, but take care not to detach the meat completely.

Freezing oysters (and clams) for half an hour before shucking (this won't freeze the shellfish inside) is said to make them much easier to open.

Silverside

A type of smelt. See **smelt**.

Skate   L   105 raie/cartilagenous

A flat, scaleless and boneless fish (being cartilaginous it has gristle rather than bones), which is usually sold skinned and

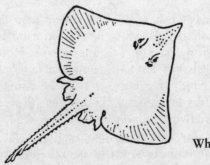

White skate

dressed as 'wings'. Don't be surprised if your skate wing has a slight smell of ammonia, this is normal and can be removed by soaking the fish for half an hour in salted water. And don't be alarmed if the fishmonger tells you the skate is a couple of days old – it is one of the few fish that is better at two days than fresh from the water. The traditional skate dish is au beurre noir – poached very gently in a simple wine vinegar **court-bouillon**, then served with foaming browned butter to which capers have been added. Some chefs like to swirl a little vinegar around the pan that the butter has been browned in and, when boiling, pour that over the skate, beurre noir and capers. A less calorific way of having your skate with capers is to grill it and serve with a pat of savoury caper butter.

Skate also makes an interesting salad: Poach it in a wine vinegar **court-bouillon**, cool and pull the flesh off in long thin strips. Arrange these on a salad of mixed leaves and pour over **tarragon vinaigrette**.

Skate livers are also considered a delicacy: the Belgians, when they can get them, simmer them gently in a little butter and spread them on toast with a dash of lemon juice.

Skinning

To skin a whole flat fish, make an incision just above the tail, and with a sharp knife ease up the skin until there is enough to get a firm grasp of. Salt fingers well. Holding tail firmly against bench with left hand, pull skin swiftly towards head with right hand. If you are not strong enough to do this, ease skin off by laying knife flat between flesh and skin and work with a sawing motion towards the head.

To skin a fillet, lay fillet skin side down on a flat surface. Insert knife at an angle between flesh and skin, grasp tail with salted fingers and with a sawing motion work towards head, pulling skin towards you and against the pressure of the knife.

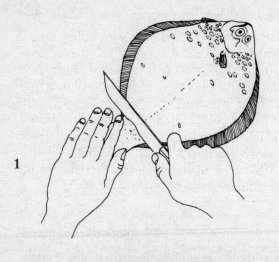

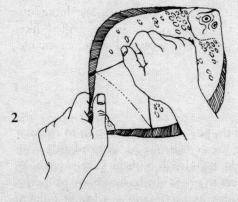

Skinning a flat fish:

1 Cut through the skin across the base of the tail and, with the point of a knife, pry the skin loose.
2 Salt fingers, then grasp the skin firmly in one hand, holding the tail with the other hand. Pull the skin towards the head. In stubborn cases, pliers might help.

Skorthalia   HC

The Greek version of **Rouille**, thickened with either bread, or potatoes or both: *Soak 3 thick slices of bread in a little water and then squeeze out any excess moisture. Place in a blender with 6 cloves of finely chopped garlic, and mix to a smooth paste. Without switching off the blender, gradually add $\frac{1}{4}$ pint (1.5 dl) olive oil, then add 2 tablespoons lemon juice, salt and black pepper to taste. If the sauce needs thickening, add more moistened bread.* Skorthalia is very tasty, but, like Aioli, it is high in calories and should be used sparingly by slimmers.

Smelt   220 eperlan/lean, round

Small slender fish about six inches long that are usually eaten, bones and all. In France, little ones are hung on skewers and deep-fried. Larger ones can be grilled like **sardines,** or stewed like tiny eels with red wine, rosemary and thyme.

Smoked Fish

When buying smoked fish, pay as much attention to quality as if you were buying fresh fish. Good smoked fish will have a bright shiny surface and will be firm to the touch. If it is dull or soggy, then it probably hasn't been properly smoked. You cannot judge by the colour – a bright golden cod or haddock fillet will probably indicate it has been dyed. Many supermarkets now indicate which smoked fish have been dyed and which haven't. Smoked fish is extremely versatile: it can be used on its own as a part of a smoked fish platter; raw in smoked fish tartare; mixed with butter or cream cheese or a mixture of fromage frais and cream cheese in a **pâté**; served uncooked or marinated in salads, or cooked in a variety of different ways from the simple, like **kedgeree** to the rather glamorous **Omelette** Arnold Bennet or Smoked Fish Gratinée.

Smoked Fish Platter: *Take several different smoked fish of varying colours and textures (mackerel, trout, eel, halibut – if you can get it – and salmon), slice them very thinly and arrange them around a scooped out half lemon filled with horseradish sauce. Serve with slices of fresh brown bread.*

Smoked Fish Tartare: This recipe uses smoked haddock, but it works well with smoked cod: *Skin, fillet and chop into tiny pieces 8 oz (200 g) smoked white fish, mix with 1 tablespoon of mayonnaise and 1 tablespoon of sour cream or yoghurt, the juice of ½ lime or lemon, 1 very finely diced tomato, and 6 chopped coriander leaves. Shape into small patties, like little hamburgers – if you have metal cookie-cutting rings, these will help to make the shape. Chill and serve with liquidised, well-chilled, fresh* **tomato** *coulis.*

Smoked Fish Pâté: *Mix 8 oz (200 g) skinned and boned smoked mackerel or kipper with 1 clove of finely crushed garlic, 2 oz (50 g) of softened butter, 1 tablespoon of lemon juice, a dash of tabasco and salt and pepper to taste, until it makes a thick smooth paste. Chill well and serve with tiny triangles of hot brown toast.*

Smoked Fish Salad: *Poached, cooled and flaked smoked haddock can be used in a Waldorf Salad with chopped apple, celery and nuts mixed together in a* **yoghurt** *and mint dressing.*

Smoked Fish Gratinée: *Cooked smoked fish can make a simple smoked fish pie in a white sauce with a potato topping or this more elegant supper dish, which requires 8 oz (200 g) of finnan haddock, 6 oz (150 g) smoked mackerel, and 4 oz (100 g) smoked trout. Poach haddock for 3 minutes, then flake the flesh into a large ovenproof* dish setting aside the skin and bones you have removed for fish stock. Add flaked trout, also setting aside skin and bones. Add flaked **mackerel**. In a separate pan simmer ¼ pint (1.5 dl) cider and ¼ pint (1.5 dl) water with a slice of onion and a small garlic clove. Add the fish skin and bones to make a fish stock. Remove from the heat, cool and strain. Next, make a thick roux from 1 tablespoon butter and 2 tablespoons flour, mix in the fish stock, stirring continuously (see **velouté**), and bring to the boil. Then simmer for 15 minutes, stirring occasionally. Add ¼ pint (1.5 dl) single cream, a pinch of ground ginger, and salt and pepper to taste. Pour this sauce over the fish, sprinkle with 2 tablespoons breadcrumbs mixed with 2 tablespoons grated parmesan cheese. Bake at 400° F/205° C/Gas Mark 6 for 15 minutes or until the top is crisp. Garnish with fresh parsley.

Sole

See under **Dover Sole** or **Lemon Sole**.

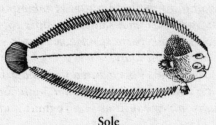

Sole

Sorrel

A cousin of the spinach, sorrel is a most useful vegetable when it comes to fish cookery: it can be used in soups, in stuffings (especially for freshwater fish like **carp**), and as a sauce. To make a creamy sorrel sauce you will need: *8 oz (200 g) sorrel, washed well, and blanched quickly in boiling water then sweated slowly over a low heat in a covered pan with 1 oz (25 g) of butter until it is almost a purée. Liquidize either in a blender or by pushing through a sieve. Add a tablespoon of fish* **stock** *(or white wine if you have no fish stock), stir well, then add 2 tablespoons of single cream (or slightly sweetened yoghurt) plus salt and pepper to taste. Heat but do not boil.*

If you simply want a bed of sorrel on which to bake your fish fillets en papillote: *Wash a generous handful of sorrel leaves (they reduce to very little), blanch and sweat in 1 teaspoon of butter in a covered pan until all moisture from the leaves has evaporated. Then, place the softened sorrel beneath the fish to be baked.*

Soufflé

Next time you are in France, buy a jar of a really good Soupe de Poisson. When you get home don't make it up as soup, turn it into a fish soufflé. It is very simple – and very effective: *You need just under 1 pint (500 ml) of strong, rich fish soup mixed with 2 tablespoons cornflour, heated until boiling and then cooled. Beat 8 egg whites until they are stiff enough to form peaks, then fold them into the thickened soup. Pour this mixture either into 4 individual buttered soufflé dishes or a large dish and cook for 12–15 minutes in a pre-heated oven at 400° F/200° C/Gas Mark 6. As with all soufflés, make sure everyone is sitting down waiting for it.*

A more traditional soufflé can be made out of almost any cooked fish, smoked fish or shellfish. But do remember that flavouring (herbs and spices) and seasoning needs to be much stronger than usual because of the blandness of the eggs. The basic recipe for a fish or shellfish soufflé is as follows: *8 oz (200 g) of puréed fish, mixed with ¼ pint (1.5 dl) thick* **béchamel sauce,** *mixed with 3 beaten egg yolks, to which is added 3 stiffly beaten egg whites (use 4 if the eggs are small). Mix together lightly but do not beat, then add this mixture to a buttered soufflé dish, filling the dish to within ½ inch of the top. Depending on the flavour of the fish, you could sprinkle 1 oz of grated parmesan cheese on top. A greaseproof paper 'collar' tied around the soufflé dish, extending a good 2 inches above the dish, will encourage your soufflé to rise. Cook at 350° F/175° C/Gas Mark 4 for 20–25 minutes. For a really rich soufflé, say of smoked salmon or crab, for cream, substitute half the béchamel liquid.*

Soup

A fish soup can either be a bisque (which is a purée of shellfish), a velouté (which is basically a smooth creamy blend of fish or shellfish and a rich sauce **velouté**) or a soupe. A soupe, unlike a **Bouillabaisse, Bourride,** or **Cioppino** does not come with or accompanied by chunks of fish and shellfish. A real Soupe de Poisson is a rich, orangey-reddish broth, thick with the flavour of all the fish that have been cooked within it but extracted before serving. Served with **Rouille,** croûtons and grated cheese (plus some fresh, French bread to mop up any leftovers), it is a light lunch or supper dish all in itself. There are a number of different recipes involving different fish or fish heads. Here is Dominique's Fish Soup made with red mullet. If you can't get fresh red mullet, frozen mullet is quite acceptable for a fish soup: *Sweat 1 sliced leek, 1 large chopped celery stalk, 1 chopped onion, 1 chopped carrot and 1 large crushed clove of garlic in 2 tablespoons of olive oil for 2–3 minutes. Add the red mullet and cook gently for 5 minutes. Add ¼ (1.5 dl) bottle* *white wine, 3 pints (18 dl) of good fish stock, 2 tablespoons tomato purée, a pinch of thyme, a bay leaf, 1 tablespoon chopped parsley, salt, pepper, a dash of cayenne pepper and a whole crab. Bring this to the boil and simmer for 1 hour. Lift out the red mullet and crab, remove the flesh from fish and crab meat from the shell and purée very finely through a sieve or in a blender. Strain the remaining liquid, then add the fish meat and crab purée, together with a good pinch of saffron. Check seasoning, reheat then serve with small dishes of* **Rouille**, *croûtons and grated cheese on the side.*

Souse

Soused fish has usually been cooked in onion, spices and vinegar, or in a mixture of wine and vinegar, in a very slow oven, then cooled and served cold. Oily fish like herrings, sardines and mackerel lend themselves to sousing, though a semi-oily fish like trout also souses well. It is a very good way of keeping a mackerel for several days, to serve with summer salads. The French call it **Mackerel** au Vin Blanc, which sounds a little more glamorous, than soused mackerel.

Spices

Fish cookery tends to lean more towards herbs than spices, as many spices can overpower the delicate flavour of fish. Ginger and saffron are two essential spices for modern fish cooking; others that are useful to have on the spice rack are: cayenne, cloves, curry, mace, nutmeg, paprika, turmeric and vanilla pod.

Spinach   27

Not only is spinach high in those good-for-you minerals, iron and potassium, it is also noted, in medical circles, for its laxative qualities. Aside from all these benefits, it is easy to cook and makes an excellent stuffing for fish in dishes like paupiettes of **plaice**; a colourful addition to fish terrines; a pretty purée for plain grilled, poached or baked fish when it is sweated in a little butter and liquidized with fresh chopped herbs; and perfect parcel wrappings for all kinds of fish, from whole fish steaks sprinkled with herbs to a kedgeree mix of smoked fish, cooked rice, chopped hard-boiled egg and a dash of turmeric, blended together with a little cream. To make a spinach parcel: *Cut off the spinach stalk, wash thoroughly and blanch for 1 minute in boiling salted water. Allow to cool. Then, place the well-seasoned and herbed fish steak or fish mix in the centre of the leaf, fold it up so that the fish is completely sealed in, tie with thread, and place in a well-buttered baking dish. Sprinkle with lemon juice and 2 tablespoons of white wine mixed with 2 tablespoons of fish* **fumet***, if you have it. If not, just add a little more wine. Cover with foil and bake according to* **Canadian Theory.**

Sprat   O   216 esprot/round

Resemble small herrings, usually about 3 inches in length, with blue backs and bright silver bellies. Can be grilled, or soused in vinegar and water. Often served smoked.

Squid   L   95 encornet/cephalopod

The squid is an inexpensive and under-rated seafood that seems to appear most often fried in oily rings, or as part of an Italian seafood salad. It can rise to much greater heights – especially in some of the pretty squid salads that are now being created, where it is cut into strips, rather than circles. One of the most appealing recipes is squid strips gently poached with sesame seeds: *Cut a squid in half lengthways and then into strips (see skinning instructions below). Heat 3½ fl oz (100 ml) good olive oil with 1¾ fl oz (50 ml) balsamic vinegar (vinegar that has been aged for two years in old wine casks – available from most good delicatessens), 1¾ fl oz (50 ml) white wine vinegar, salt and pepper and 1 tablespoon of sesame seeds, until the seeds turn golden-brown. Add the strips of squid, stir well and remove from heat. Cool and chill. Add a dash of lime juice, extra salt and pepper if necessary. Arrange squid on a bed of mixed lettuce leaves, pour over the liquid and garnish with toasted sesame seeds. The golden squid looks even better if it is combined with chilled, cooked octopus tentacles turned a rosy pink by simmering them in red wine or tomatoes.*

Squid

If you prefer your squid tube whole, try it stuffed with a spicy mix of olives, anchovies and chillies: *Stuff 4 cleaned squid tubes with a mushy mixture of ½ a chopped french bread stick, 8 chopped black olives, 6 anchovy fillets, 2 garlic cloves, 2 hot chillies, 1 tablespoon chopped parsley, and ½ cup olive oil. Charcoal grill for 1 minute on each side and sprinkle lightly with balsamic vinegar and olive oil before serving.*

Preparing squid:

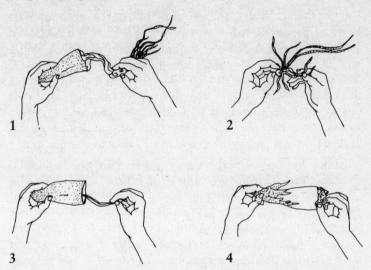

1

2

3   4

If you can't persuade your fishmonger to prepare your squid for you here's how:

1 Remove the head, tentacles and intestines from the hood.
2 Grasp the tentacles at the base and press firmly, so that the beak pops out. Discard the beak and set the tentacles aside.
3 Grasp the tube and slide out the quill-like translucent membrane.
4 Remove fins with fingers or a knife. Then remove the speckled skin from the head by peeling it back and pulling firmly.
5 Rinse the tube thoroughly and pat dry. To soften, place it in a plastic bag with a peeled kiwi fruit for 30 minutes, or blanch for 2 minutes in boiling water.

Steam

One of the healthiest, and certainly one of the least fattening ways of preparing fish is to steam it. Steamed fish is cooked by being suspended above a small amount of boiling water (or fish stock) inside a closed container. The perfect answer is a purpose-designed fish steamer large enough to take the grandest of fish, but these are extremely expensive. Less costly (though still not cheap) and tremendously useful for fish up to 1 foot long or various cuts of fish, are the multi-layered electric steamers. These can cook fish and vegetables together on separate layers and can be used for vegetables or ravioli when you are not eating fish. At the time of writing, the cheapest of these was around £30.00. However it is quite easy to steam fish without a special steamer. You can make your own steamer by placing one of those collapsible wire vegetable baskets inside a large closed saucepan; by putting a low wire cake cooling-rack inside a large baking dish and covering it with foil; by inserting a wire rack inside your wok, or even by standing a metal colander on top of a coffee cup inside a very large lidded saucepan – just as long as the fish doesn't touch the water, as there is room for the steam to swirl around the fish, and as long as the lid or cover is tight enough to keep the steam from escaping these methods will work. Almost any fish or shellfish can be steamed – provided it fits in your steamer. For successful steaming:

1 Place fish on top of a small lightly-buttered plate or piece of oiled foil on the steaming rack. This will prevent the fish juices from falling into the water below.
2 Season fish well, inside and out, using more herbs than for other cooking methods.

3 If fish is delicate, wrap it in lettuce leaves or seaweed sheets to protect it.

4 Use no more than 1 inch of liquid for fish and $\frac{1}{2}$ inch for shellfish.

5 Try steaming in fish stock and wine for extra flavour, or add herbs to the water.

6 Time the fish according to the **Canadian Theory**.

Stew

Fish dishes with a high liquid content like Bouillabaisse, Bourride, and Cioppino are sometimes called soups and sometimes stews – there is no hard and fast rule. Soups are not generally thickened, though fish stews, like the Spanish **Zarzuela**, are usually made thicker with a little flour and water.

Stock

Making your own fish stock may sound a bit of a hassle, but it is worth the effort. Once prepared, you can use it as a base for soups, stews, and sauces and for adding flavour to other fish dishes. Once strained and reduced into a **fumet**, it will keep in the refrigerator for several days or it can be frozen. To make your fumet, reduce fish stock by boiling it vigorously over a high heat until it is reduced in volume by about half, thus considerably concentrating the flavour.

A simple fish stock can be made from the following: *1 oz (25 g) butter, melted in a large saucepan, 1 sliced onion, 1 sliced carrot, 2 sliced sticks celery, and, if you have it, the white part of 1 sliced leek. Soften these together for 5 minutes, then add 2 lbs (800 g) of fish trimmings (bones, tails and off-cuts, but make sure there are no gills), and sweat these for 2 minutes. Add a bay leaf, several large*

*parsley sprigs, a few black peppercorns, a pinch of dried
thyme, a tablespoon of white wine vinegar, ½ pint (3 dl)
white wine and 3 pints (18 dl) of water. Bring to the boil,
simmer for 30 minutes, then strain. Keep to use as stock or
reduce by at least half to use as a fumet for sauces.*

Storing

Fish straight from the water tastes indescribably better than
fish that is even a day old. But very few people have the
opportunity to eat fish that is anywhere near that fresh.
Given the complicated chain of fishing boat to fish auction
to fish market to fishmonger, fish is usually getting on for 2
days old by the time it gets to you – but there is nothing
wrong with this. Tests by the Massachusetts Marine Fisheries Department show that a whole fresh fish can keep for 7
to 10 days without being frozen, provided it is gutted, gilled
and stored in a container in the refrigerator on a bed of
crushed ice. The ice should be drained and replaced when
necessary. If you are not storing fish on a bed of ice, then a
whole fish (again, gutted, gilled, and washed and dried well)
should keep for 2–3 days wrapped in foil. Steaks or fillets
will also keep for 2–3 days in your refrigerator, provided
they are wrapped in leakproof plastic bags, preferably two
bags, in case the first one punctures. Smoked fish should be
loosely wrapped in foil and used within 5 days. Shelled
mussels, clams and oysters should be used in 2 days, as
should cooked shellfish. However, cooked shellfish can be
frozen for up to 3 months.

Always keep fish in the coldest part of the refrigerator:
the optimum temperature is 32° F, and should never rise
above 40° F.

Stuffing

Medium-sized round fish like mullet, bream, snapper and
trout are the easiest fish to stuff, but it is possible (though
rather fiddly) to stuff small fish like sardines and flat fish
such as lemon sole and flounder. You will need to scale, gill
and gut the fish first, and you may also want to bone it,
though this is not necessary. Rinse the fish inside and out
under cold running water and dry. Season fish inside and
out with salt, pepper and lemon juice and brush the inside
of the stuffing cavity with melted butter or oil. Distribute
the stuffing evenly along the middle of the fish, making sure
it is not over-stuffed and that the two sides will close. Bring
the belly flaps together and close in one of the following
ways:

1 Tie with twine at intervals along the body of the fish.
2 Sew up the two sides with large needle and thread.
3 Bring the belly flaps together and pierce them at
   intervals with metal skewers, then, in a zig-zag fashion,
   wind a cotton thread around the skewers as though
   you were lacing up an old-fashioned boot.

Fish can then be wrapped in foil and baked according to
the **Canadian Theory.**

Fish stuffings can vary from a simple mixture of chopped
herbs or vegetables to proper bread-based, egg-bound stuffings: 6 oz (150 g) *sliced mushrooms and 1 small onion,
finely chopped, sweated in 1 oz (25 g) butter till soft. Mix in
a bowl with 4 oz (100 g) fresh breadcrumbs, 1 teaspoon
thyme, ½ teaspoon sage, a generous tablespoon of freshly
chopped parsley, 1 tablespoon lemon juice and 1 large beaten
egg yolk. To this stuffing mixture you can add a variety of
flavours: 1 tablespoon chopped anchovies; 6 oz (150 g)*

chopped shrimps or prawns; 3–8 tablespoons spinach or
sorrel, softened in a little butter, then puréed (try adding a
generous grating of nutmeg); a 4 inch piece cucumber, diced;
2 tablespoons chopped stoned olives; 2 tablespoons chopped
fennel (softened first in a little butter); or even 3 tablespoons
minced oysters or baby clams. Many Middle Eastern recipes
use cooked rice as the base for a stuffing instead of bread-
crumbs, see **bream.**

Sturgeon   L   102 esturgeon/round

A very meaty fish that is often compared to veal. Fresh
sturgeon is only very occasionally available to this country,
and even frozen is not all that common. It is found more
frequently in France, a by-product of the small Bordeaux

Sturgeon

caviar industry. Smoked sturgeon is quite delicious and can
be found in a few superior delicatessens. Should you find
yourself with a frozen sturgeon steak, braise it well in wine
and herbs as **tuna.**

Suppion   L   95 sepiole/cephalopod

Baby cuttlefish never more than two inches long, usually
less. Usually eaten fried.

Sunfish   poisson lune/round, oily

A rare semi-tropical visitor to our shores during very warm
summers. Also known as the Opah, or the moonfish, it is
brilliantly coloured in scarlet, blue, green and purple. Sunfish
can grow to at least 100 lb and is usually cut into steaks and
treated like tuna. Some say it tastes like salmon, only mea-
tier. Braise as **tuna**.

Surimi

Boned, minced fish with much of the moisture removed.
Used commercially to make mock crab or scampi products.

Sushi

Sushi are small rolls or bars consisting of thin slices of raw
fish wrapped around, or inside vinegared rice, and often
bound by thin sheets of seaweed. They are usually seasoned
with wasabi, a hot green horseradish, and are always served
in pairs, generally to be eaten in the hand – not with
chopsticks. The first sushi roll was allegedly created in a
similar manner to the English sandwich. An eighteenth
century Japanese gambler called for something to eat in his
hand so that he wouldn't have to interrupt his gaming. The
chef wrapped a piece of tuna inside a roll of vinegared rice,
bound it with seaweed and called it Tekka Maki ('Maki'
meaning roll) after the Tekkaba Gambling House. The
Tekka Maki is traditionally included in a Sushi platter.

Sushi-making is regarded as a highly skilled art, com-
bining creativity with culinary technique. Most Japanese
Sushi chefs need a five year apprenticeship, so don't worry
if it takes you a while to get the hang of it. There are a
number of excellent Japanese cookbooks with detailed instructions on how to create a range of sushi.

Swordfish   O   136 espadon/round

Now they have declared that swordfish is not dangerously loaded with mercury (as was once believed) but instead, is full of beneficial Omega 3, it is becoming increasingly popular world-wide. Once only available frozen in steaks, it is sometimes now available fresh.

Swordfish has a firm white flesh that lends itself admirably to grilling and barbequing, and is much improved by a little marinading in wine, oil and herbs before grilling as steaks or kebabs: *Cut 1 lb (400 g) swordfish into cubes and marinate for 1 hour in 4 tablespoons olive oil, 2 tablespoons lemon or lime juice, 1 teaspoon each chopped dill and parsley, salt and pepper. Lift out of the marinade and sprinkle with paprika and cayenne, thread on skewers with peppers and onions and grill until golden-brown.* Swordfish steaks are delicious with black olive **butter** or with an anchovy **sauce**.

Tail

The tail is usually left on during the cooking of a whole fish, but you may have to cover it with foil to make sure it doesn't burn during cooking, given that it is so much thinner than the rest of the fish.

Tapenade

An anchovy and olive purée from Provence that can be used as a dip for raw vegetables, a sauce for cold fish, or a savoury spread for toasted French bread: *Mix 1 lb (400 g) of stoned black olives in a blender together with 1 large chopped garlic clove, 4 oz (100 g) of drained anchovy fillets, 1 oz (25 g) capers, fresh ground black pepper and 2 tablespoons olive oil.*

There are a number of different versions of this – some recipes add 2 oz (50 g) of flaked tuna, some add 2 tablespoons cognac, some use less olives, some less garlic. Tapenade will keep in a screwtop jar in the fridge for weeks – the amount given here would be enough to provide canapés or a dip for 12 people, as it is fairly strong, and should be used sparingly.

Taramasalata

Can be made with salted grey mullet roe, carp roe or more commonly with smoked cod's roe: *Immerse a 4 oz (100 g) piece of smoked cod roe briefly in boiling water, then remove the skin with a knife. Soak the skinned roe for at least 1 hour to remove some of the saltiness. Then moisten a thick slice of crustless bread in a little water so that it becomes completely soggy, then place it in a blender with 2 crushed cloves of garlic and the roe. Blend together well, then add 1 beaten egg yolk and blend again. Then slowly add ½ pint (3 dl) of olive oil, in a thin steady stream, as if you were making mayonnaise. Finally, add the strained juice of 1 lemon. If the taramasalata is too thin, add a little more lightly-moistened bread and blend again.* Serve with hot toast or, for a more authentic approach, with hot pitta bread.

Tarragon

If you have space on your window ledge for only a few fresh herbs, make sure that tarragon is one of them; after parsley and dill, it is one of the most useful herbs in fish cooking. Make sure the plant you buy is French rather than Russian tarragon, as the latter has very little taste. Add it with parsley to mayonnaise, to make **green sauce**: *Chop 2 tablespoons into ½ pint (3 dl)* **vinaigrette** *for a tarragon vinaigrette and transform a skate salad.* Make tarragon butter to garnish plain grilled fish: *Mix 2 tablespoons with 4 oz (100 g) softened butter and 1 tablespoon of lemon juice.* Or make a tarragon cream sauce, delicious on trout, as follows: *Simmer 4 heaped tablespoons of fresh chopped tarragon in 3 tablespoons dry white wine, till the wine has almost evaporated. Then, add ½ pint (3 dl) of* **béchamel** sauce, *heat and stir in a walnut-sized knob of butter just before serving.*

Tartare

LC

Fish served à la tartare is raw fish usually moulded into a small pattie. Salmon and **tuna** are the fish most often found tartared on restaurant menus, but occasionally you find something different, like **smoked fish**, or **scallops**. A good bet for weight watchers, since there are hardly any additions to fish served in this way.

Tartare Sauce

The perfect accompaniment to cold shellfish and fish dishes, provided it's not the bottled variety which is nothing like the real thing. Good tartare sauce should be made from: *½ pint (3 dl) mayonnaise, to which is added 2 chopped cloves of garlic, 1 tablespoon chopped gherkin, 1 tablespoon chopped spring onion, 1 tablespoon chopped parsley, 1 tablespoon chopped capers, and 1 teaspoon of lemon juice.*

Tempura

This is the Japanese method of deep-frying fish and vege-tables in very hot oil in a very light batter. Prawns, squid and very small whole fish work well under the tempura treatment. The secret of successful tempura is hidden in the batter – it must be very light: *Beat 1 large egg yolk, gradually add ½ pint (3 dl) iced water, beating occasionally, then add 8 oz (200 g) of sifted flour, but stir very lightly. The batter should look lumpy, as though it is not properly mixed. Use immediately. Score prawns several times across the belly to stop them curling, then coat them with flour. Dip the prawns*

*first into batter then into the hot oil, which should be
maintained at about 350° F/175° C. When barely golden,
remove from the oil and drain on paper towels. Tempura
prawns can be served with a dip made of soy sauce mixed
with a little* **dashi** *(Japanese fish stock) and a little mirin
(sweet cooking sake) or sake with sugar added to taste.*

Tench $\boxed{O}$ 140 tanche/round

A greeny-bronze freshwater fish generally found in slow-
moving rivers. Much more popular around the Loire and its
tributaries, than in this country. In France they frequently
stuff it with a mixture of hard-boiled egg, mushrooms,
parsley, bay and breadcrumbs, then bake it slowly in white
wine. Tench is also poached in a **court-bouillon,** then served
with a red wine **butter** made by softening a chopped shallot
in butter and adding well-reduced red wine. The easiest way
to scale a tench is to dip it in boiling water first.

Terrine

A thick chunky pâté cooked in an earthenware dish called a
terrine. The terrine is usually placed for cooking in a large
baking tin half-filled with warm water, and frequently has a
weighted lid to prevent the contents rising. Most fish and
shellfish can be used in terrines. See **Whiting** and crab terrine. Whiting is ideal when the recipe calls for 'a pound of
white fish fillets'.

Thyme

A particularly aromatic herb, which is generally considered
too strong to be used on its own with most fish, except

perhaps very meaty fish like tuna and shark. It is useful, however, as an ingredient in a bouquet garni for stocks, soups and stews and as a flavouring for **stuffings**.

Tilapia   ☐L round

Type of bream extensively farmed in the Sea of Galilee and now in France. Also called St Peter fish, because of the splodgy black 'thumbprint'. Treat as **bream**.

Tomato   14

The essential ingredient for many fish soups, stews and sauces, but at its best in a simple fresh tomato sauce which can turn a cod kebab or plain grilled fish into something quite delicious. The following recipe for fresh tomato sauce or coulis is one of the simplest, provided you can keep an eye on it while it is reducing: *Heat 1 small finely sliced onion very gently in ½ oz (12 g) butter and 1 tablespoon olive oil until golden. Add 1½ lbs (600 g) very ripe chopped tomatoes, 1 teaspoon of salt, 1 teaspoon of sugar, 1 clove of chopped garlic, 1 teaspoon of chopped parsley, 2 large chopped basil leaves or a little dried basil and simmer all together for 20 minutes before liquidizing in a blender. If it is at all watery, place the mixture back in the pan and simmer till all water has gone. Season to taste – it may need a little more sugar.*

Tope

Species of **shark**.

Trimmings

The pieces left over when a fish has been filleted – the bones, the head, the tail, the fins are the trimmings. They can all be used to make a fish stock, but if the head is to be included make sure it has been thoroughly cleaned and the gills have been removed, or the stock will have a rather bitter taste.

Trout $\boxed{O}$ 150 truite/round

There is frequently some confusion, exacerbated by the odd unscrupulous restaurateur, over which trout are 'salmon trout' and which are farmed rainbow trout. Sea trout or salmon trout which lives in salt water, and the brown trout which lives in fresh water are all first cousins – members of the 'salmo trutta' family. The rainbow trout with its dark spotted tail belongs to a different family altogether – the salmo gairdneri, which was introduced into the UK from the US to provide stock for the trout farmers and the anglers. The colour of its flesh depends on what the farmer is feeding it on. The salmon or sea trout has the superior flavour and can generally be used in all recipes calling for salmon.

Trout

Trout is quite delicious marinated, especially when done in a hazelnut **vinaigrette** and scattered with pretty pink peppercorns: *Arrange 8 oz (200 g) thinly sliced raw pink salmon trout on a platter. 30 minutes before serving, pour over a mixture of 3 tablespoons hazelnut oil, 2 tablespoons* *lemon juice, and salt and pepper. Cover with foil and chill. To serve, sprinkle with pink peppercorns and sprigs of fresh dill.* Pink peppercorns are available from good delicatessens.

Rainbow trout are also ideal for baking in foil: *Try sprinkling the inside and outside with a little brown sugar and freshly chopped mint, before moistening with wine and sealing foil; or lay trout on foil, season inside and out, and around it on the foil, place 2 cloves, 2 crumbled bay leaves, a strip of lemon peel, 1 small sliced onion and several sprigs of parsley. Dot with a little butter, moisten liberally with white wine, seal the foil and bake. Serve hot with parsley* **butter** *or cold with herb* **mayonnaise.**

For a special lunch, poach trout in a **court-bouillon** made with rosé wine, then add gelatine to make a pretty pink Trout in Rosé **Aspic.** Cold trout can also be served as **Escabèche.**

Tuna $\boxed{O}$ 165 thon/round

Tuna is another high-fashion fish that was once available in this country only as frozen steaks, but which is now increasingly sold fresh to meet the demand for sushi and the

Tuna

variety of raw and marinated tuna dishes such as **Carpaccio** and Tuna Tartare: *Dice very finely, or pass through a meat mincer, 1 lb (400 g) very fresh tuna fillets that have been skinned and boned. Cover with film or foil and chill. 1 hour before serving, add 2 tablespoons olive oil, 2 beaten egg* *yolks, 2 drops tabasco, 1 tablespoon finely chopped capers, 1 tablespoon finely chopped parsley, 1 tablespoon finely chopped dill pickle, 1 tablespoon finely chopped shallots, ½ tablespoon Dijon mustard, salt and pepper to the tuna. Serve in small mounds on a chilled fresh* **tomato coulis**.

Cooked tuna is a very meaty looking fish – perfect for serving to those who claim not to like fish, and even better if it is casseroled with red wine (the flavour is full enough to warrant it): *Spike a large piece of tuna (about 1½ lbs (600 g) or 4 large tuna steaks (frozen will serve the purpose) with 8 anchovy fillets, poking them in and out of the tuna flesh with a sharp knife. In a frying-pan, brown 1 large thinly sliced onion in 2 tablespoons olive oil, then place the fish in the pan to seal it on both sides in the oil for 2 or 3 minutes. Add 1 × 15 oz (375 g) tin drained peeled tomatoes and their juice, ½ pint red (or white) wine and enough tomato juice to cover. Close and cook very slowly on top of the stove for about 45 minutes. For a fuller flavour, add a little thyme or rosemary. Before serving, sprinkle with chopped parsley, finely grated lemon zest and finely chopped garlic.* Also try: *Tuna steaks marinated in 2 tablespoons olive oil and 1 table-spoon of chopped mint for 1 hour, grilled and served with a warm* **mint vinaigrette**.

Turbot　　　　　　　　　　　　　　　L　112 turbot/flat

Regarded, and rightly so, as the king of the flat fish, the turbot has such a firm-textured, but delicate-flavoured flesh, that, like the lily, it needs little gilding. It is perfectly suited to steaming or poaching, assuming you have a pan big enough for a whole turbot. If you do not, don't rush out and purchase a purpose-built turbotière – they are fiendishly expensive. Rather make yourself a steaming dish by placing a wire cooling rack inside a large baking dish and covering the dish with foil. As long as the turbot is not touching the liquid, and the steam from the liquid is not escaping from the dish, this do-it-yourself arrangement will work. Steam over a **court-bouillon** and serve with a gentle hollandaise, or perhaps a light **saffron** sauce. Little turbot are called chicken turbot and can be plain grilled like small **dover sole**.

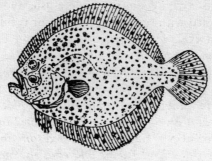

Turbot

Turbot is another fish that is well-suited to serving raw: *Try it in very thin slices marinated for at least 6 hours in a mixture of 2 tablespoons sherry vinegar, 3 tablespoons walnut oil, 4 chopped tomatoes, salt and pepper blended all together. Add a dash of lemon or lime juice, and serve garnished with a* **julienne** *of seeded tomatoes and chopped basil leaves.*

Vanilla

A flavour much more associated with confectionery than fish cookery, but which works surprisingly well with **lobster** – in a lobster, vanilla and green bean salad – and equally well with the fish they call mock lobster, the **monkfish**, in the same salad. There are no calories in vanilla.

Velouté

Velouté means velvety or smooth and in fish cuisine refers either to a thick **sauce** made from a white roux and fish stock, or a creamy fish soup as in Sole Velouté.

Vermouth 35

A white wine flavoured with, among other things, cinnamon, coriander, cloves and elderberries. Vermouth goes particularly well with shellfish and some crustacea, and is occasionally found as the dominant flavour in sauce for white fish – dover sole is sometimes served in a cream and vermouth sauce.

Vermouth also perks up a fish stock – try adding 2 table-spoons to a ½ pint (3 dl) of stock – and gives an interesting flavour to a fish steak that is about to be baked in foil. If you are right out of white wine but have a bottle of ver-mouth handy, you could use it in most recipes in place of white wine, provided you cut down the quantity by a good half. There are approximately 35 calories in 1 fl oz (25 ml) vermouth, though this can vary according to sweetness.

Vinaigrette

A mixture of oil, vinegar, salt and pepper, vinaigrette is a wonderful base from which to create light and imaginative cold fish sauces – from a simple tarragon vinaigrette for cold skate salad, to a basil and tomato vinaigrette on grilled scallops, from an orange and lemon vinaigrette on chilled prawns to a raspberry vinaigrette for a salad of **john dory**.

For a simple vinaigrette: *Crush very finely 1 small clove of garlic, and add with a generous pinch of salt and good grinding of black pepper to 1 tablespoon of good quality wine vinegar. Add 5 tablespoons of very good olive oil and mix thoroughly. If you don't have a blender, put it into a screwtop jar with a very firm lid and shake it hard. It makes sense to mix up more than enough for one meal – just re-member to stick to the basic proportions of five parts oil and one part vinegar. If you don't much care for garlicky dressing, leave out the garlic.*

To make a tarragon vinaigrette: *Add 2 heaped tablespoons chopped tarragon to a cup of the basic vinaigrette. Use the same proportions for other herbs.*

For the orange and lemon vinaigrette: *Substitute 1 table-spoon of lemon juice and 1 tablespoon of orange juice for the vinegar and mix in 1 tablespoon of orange zest.*

For the raspberry vinaigrette which works so well with a

john dory salad (or indeed with any salad of cold cooked lean white fish): *Take 4 fl oz (1 dl) fish stock and reduce over a high heat by* ⅔. Add 2 oz (50 g) *of fresh raspberries, 3 tablespoons of raspberry vinegar (make your own by soaking raspberries in ordinary wine vinegar for 3 or 4 days), 5 tablespoons of sesame oil (use olive oil if sesame is unavailable). Boil for several minutes. Cool. Blend well, and then pass through a fine sieve. Add salt and freshly ground black pepper before serving.*

For a tomato and basil vinaigrette: *Add to* ½ *pint (3 dl) basic vinaigrette, 1 medium peeled, seeded and very finely chopped ripe tomato and 1 heaped tablespoon of finely chopped fresh basil. This is surprisingly good on cold poached salmon.*

For a very stylish champagne vinaigrette, which is perfect on chilled **prawns**: *Mix 5 tablespoons olive oil, 1 tablespoon tarragon vinegar, 1 tablespoon white wine and a* ½ *pint (3 dl) champagne (just over a* ¼ *bottle).*

Vodka   50

The spirit most often found as an accompaniment to **Caviar** or **Gravad Lax**, served well-iced and knocked back in a single gulp. But there is one interesting raw fish salad: *Thin slices of oily fish like mackerel and salmon, and halibut – you'll need 4 oz (100 g) of each – are marinated for 1 hour in 2 good measures of vodka, the juice of* ½ *lime, a sprinkling of sea salt, black pepper and a dash of cayenne, then arranged according to colour and texture on individual plates.*

Waldorf

An apple, celery and walnut salad that works well topped with cooked, flaked smoked cod or haddock and dressed with a **yoghurt and mint** dressing: *Poach 1 lb (400 g) skinned, smoked haddock or cod fillets cut into small cubes for 3 or 4 minutes in enough fish stock to cover, or cook in 1 oz butter (25 g) for 2 to 3 minutes until cooked but not flaking. Remove fish cubes from pan, set aside to chill for 2 hours. Dice 1 large apple, 2 sticks celery and chop 1 table-spoon walnuts. Add to the chilled fish. Prepare ½ pint (3 dl)* **yoghurt mint** *dressing and mix thoroughly with fish and apple. Line a salad bowl with large lettuce leaves and pour in the Smoked Fish Waldorf. Garnish with a sprig of fresh mint and fresh ground black pepper.*

Walnut 600

Walnuts are better suited to cold fish – either as a walnut vinaigrette, replacing the olive oil in the basic **vinaigrette** with walnut oil and blending with 1 tablespoon of chopped walnuts, or as a walnut sauce, which is more like a very rich

mayonnaise and is perfect for smoked trout or smoked eel:
You will need: *4 oz (100 g) of walnuts, 4 oz (100 g) of
butter, a cup of fresh white breadcrumbs, a cup of chopped
parsley, 2 tablespoons lemon juice, 4 tablespoons single
cream, and ½ pint (3 dl) of walnut oil. Mix all ingredients
except oil in a food processor until creamy then add oil
slowly as though making mayonnaise. Add salt and pepper
to taste.* Both vinaigrette and sauce may need a touch of
sugar as some walnuts are sweeter than others. Weight
watchers should treat walnuts with caution: 1 oz (25 g)
contains almost 150 calories.

Wasabi

A green horseradish much favoured by the Japanese as
accompaniment to raw fish dishes, such as **Sashimi** and
Sushi. It is available from oriental delicatessens.

Watercress   16

Because of its brilliant green colour when puréed, watercress
is a most attractive companion to pink or white fish or
shellfish. To prepare a simple watercress puŕe: *Wash 2
bunches of watercress well. Blanch in well-salted boiling
water for 2 minutes, then plunge it quickly into very cold
water to ensure it keeps its colour. Purée in a blender or
force through a sieve, then add a dash of lemon juice, salt
and black pepper, a grating of nutmeg, and 2 tablespoons of
sour cream or yoghurt. Blend again until well mixed. If you
require a paler sauce, dilute the mixture with ¼ the amount
of well-puréed cooked potato. If you are to serve it hot, add
a knob of butter.* A pale pink, skinned smoked trout looks
very pretty sitting in a pool of vivid green watercress sauce.
Keep aside some sprigs of watercress for decoration.

Waterzooi

A stew of freshwater fish such as **Perch**.

Whelk   ♡ L 102 buccin/shellfish

Looking like a large brown snail, the common whelk deserves to be more popular when you consider the 'amatory properties' it is reputed to draw from all its minerals. Its tough, chewy texture could be responsible for its less than aphrodisiac reputation. Whelks are not to everyone's taste when bottled in vinegar, and are much easier to eat in fish soups, stews and chowders – you could use them in place of clams. Whelks are known as the scavengers of the ocean, so it is important that you avoid them anywhere the waters might be a little suspect in terms of pollution.

Whisky   50

Malt whisky is said to make all the difference to Gravad Mac, the marinated mackerel version of **Gravad Lax**.

Whitebait   O 250 round

These are the very small fry of sprats and herrings. Whitebait are usually deep-fried and served simply with brown bread and lemon juice. In Japan, they are served minced and raw with a little **wasabi**. Try them as whitebait fritters: *Make a batter with 1 tablespoon self-raising flour, 1 beaten egg, 2 tablespoons milk, salt and pepper to taste and add to it a cup of whitebait that have been washed and dried. Place batter in hot oil or oil and butter as though making a pancake. Turn once, drain on paper towel, serve with lemon and chopped parsley.*

Whiting   100 merlan/lean, round

A much under-rated cousin of the cod, whiting has a delicate, almost sweet-tasting flesh that is still excellent value in
these days of ever-rising fish prices. It is a little drier than its
cod or haddock relations, so is better poached or baked
with enough liquid to keep it moist, as in whiting with white
wine and olives: *Place 4 small filleted whiting in an ovenproof dish. Pour over 2 tablespoons olive oil and 4 tablespoons white wine, add a sprig of fennel, a crumbled bayleaf, and salt and pepper. Bake uncovered for 15 minutes in
a moderate oven, at 350° F/175° C/Gas Mark 4, then add a
dozen stoned black olives and cook for another 5 minutes.
Serve with slices of orange or lemon arranged along each
fish.*

Whiting can be used in any of those recipes which call for
'a pound of white fish fillets', such as fish soufflés, mousses
and terrines. In this very simple terrine, whiting blends
perfectly with a dressed crab: *Add ½ lb (200 g) skinned and
boned whiting fillet to the meat of 1 large dressed Cromer
crab. Put in a blender and mix well. Add salt, pepper and
then gradually add 2 beaten egg whites, followed by ¼ cup
cream and 4 large chopped basil leaves. Pour this mixture
into a buttered terrine. Cover with lid or foil and place in a
roasting pan half filled with boiling water. Simmer for half
an hour or till firm. Serve hot with a* **beurre blanc** *or cold
with a herb* **mayonnaise**.

Wine

A tablespoon of wine added to a humble cod steak cooked
in foil with a little lemon juice and fresh parsley will add
only 10 calories to the meal – but it can make a world of
difference to the taste. It will also improve the texture; wine

helps to break down any toughness in the fibres, so it is ideal for marinating very meaty fish like tuna and swordfish, which might otherwise be a little dry.

It won't, by the way, affect your equilibrium at all – the alcohol evaporates during the cooking process, leaving only a wonderfully concentrated flavour. The only important rule for cooking with wine is don't use any wine for cooking that you wouldn't cheerfully drink yourself. There is nothing wrong with cheap wine, but cheap nasty cooking wine (as opposed to drinking wine) can spoil a delicate fish or an otherwise delectable sauce.

Winkle   ♡ 85 bigorneau/lean, shellfish

Baby cousin of the whelk, also high in 'amatory' minerals. Usually eaten raw (winkled out on the end of a pin) but can be cooked like **mussels**.

Witch   L 100 plie grise/flat

Also known as Torbay sole and witch flounder, the witch has a pretty pale pink tinge to its skin. It can be used as **dab** or **lemon sole**, but because it is thinner than both of these, it may dry out if grilled. Small ones can be cooked à la meunière, larger ones should be oven-baked with enough liquid to keep them moist.

Wok

Given that stir-frying in a wok involves only a little added oil, it is a reasonably low-calorie method of cooking fish. Shellfish and cephalopods like squid are better suited for stir-frying than lean white fish, and a fairly bland oil, like peanut or grapeseed, is better than olive. Make sure the

pan is not over-crowded so that the heat can reach all ingredients at the same time. Remember that the stir in stir-
frying does not mean a slow circular stir, but a quick tossing
and turning movement so that food is always on the move
and cooks quickly and evenly. For stir-fried squid: *Cut
1½ lb (600 g) squid into thin 2 in (5 cm) strips, and blanch in
boiling water for 2 minutes, strain and dry. In a wok, heat
(to very hot) 2 tablespoons vegetable oil or peanut oil (not
olive oil) and stir-fry the squid very quickly. Remove and
keep warm. To the hot oil add 4 finely chopped spring
onions; I carrot, cut into very fine long strips; 1 green pepper,
cut into very fine strips; 2 stalks celery, cut in fine strips; 2
crushed cloves garlic, and 1 teaspoon finely chopped fresh
ginger root and stir fry for 2 minutes. Add 2 tablespoons
sherry and ¼ pint (1.5 dl) fish stock (or chicken stock if you
haven't any fish) and heat very quickly to reduce it to a
thick sauce. Pour this sauce over the squid and serve with
plain boiled rice.*

Wrasse   86 crenilabre/lean, round

For years consigned to the bait department, the wrasse has
only recently moved into the kitchen. A large-lipped perch-
type fish with a colourful orange-brown speckled skin, it
should be cooked like **red snapper** or ocean **perch**. An inexpensive, low-calorie fish that is worth experimenting
with.

Yoghurt

Unfortunately, no one has yet come up with a yoghurt that tastes just like cream, though someone is bound to be working on it. The creamiest of the available yoghurts is probably the strained Greek Cows' Yoghurt (not the sheeps' yoghurt which is in an identical package) and it will taste even more cream-like if you dilute it slightly with one of the low-fat enriched milks such as Vital. Even if you're not on a diet, you will probably find a yoghurt mint dressing, a yoghurt, mustard and dill dressing or a yoghurt cucumber dressing makes a refreshing addition to cold fish and fish salads. Low-fat yogurt is 15–20 calories per 1 oz (25 g), depending on the brand; Greek yoghurt is double that.

For the yoghurt mint dressing: *Mix a cup of yoghurt with 2 tablespoons chopped mint, 1 tablespoon of liquid honey and 1 teaspoon of lemon juice and chill well.*

For the yoghurt, mustard and dill dressing: *Mix 2 tablespoons of olive oil, 1 tablespoon of lemon juice, 1 tablespoon of mustard, and 1 tablespoon of finely chopped dill in a cup of yoghurt and season to taste.*

For the cucumber yoghurt dressing: *Mix a cup of yoghurt,*

1 *tablespoon parsley, the juice of* ½ *lemon, and* ½ *a cucumber, peeled, seeded and grated or diced very finely.*

Yoghurt can also be used instead of sour cream – as in baked **haddock**; instead of mayonnaise for a tuna salad sandwich: Add a little grated onion, a dash of lemon juice and some chopped parsley to the yoghurt; or it can be used as a base for a very simple **sardine** pâté.

Zarzuela |HC|

Sometimes called the Spanish answer to **Bouillabaisse**, even though it is served in many restaurants on the French sector of the Catalan coast. Zarzuela is a full rich seafood stew, made even heartier in some Catalan villages by the addition of rum instead of the usual anise, or brandy: *In 1 tablespoon of olive oil, lightly brown 2 chopped garlic cloves and 1 large chopped onion. Then add 4 peeled, seeded and chopped tomatoes or 1 × 15 oz (375 g) can of tomatoes well drained. Cook for 5 minutes and add* ¼ *pint (1.5 dl) fish stock. Add 1 tablespoon of parsley, 1 tablespoon finely chopped blanched almonds,* ¼ *teaspoon saffron, a dash of paprika, and a glass of dry white wine and leave to simmer.*

In a separate pan, in 2 tablespoons olive oil, lightly brown 1 lb (400 g) haddock or hake, cut in pieces, ½ *lb (200 g) flat fish (say lemon sole, plaice or flounder),* ½ *lb (200 g) eel in pieces, 1 squid sliced into rings, a dozen peeled prawns. Remove, drain and add to simmering stew liquid, putting the firmer fish in first. Add 24 shellfish (mussels, clams, cockles) season to taste and simmer for five minutes. Heat 2–3 tablespoons rum (or Pernod or brandy) in a small pot, set it alight and pour it, hopefully still flaming, into the stew. Stir, simmer for 2–3 minutes and serve. If you prefer a thicker stew, add 1 dessertspoon of flour mixed into a little cold water.*

ACKNOWLEDGEMENTS AND THANKS

Dr Alexander Leaf, Harvard Medical School, Boston, Massachusetts
Dr Roy Hardie, Torrie Research Institute
Alan Hulme, Torrie Research Institute
Dr Hugh Sinclair, International Nutrition Foundation
Dr Richard Cotterill, British Nutrition Foundation
Dr Tom Sanders, Kings College, London
Dr Joyce Nettleton, Lexington, Massachusetts
Simon Bossy, Agriculture and Fisheries Department, Jersey
The Sea Fish Authority, Edinburgh
Leleu and Morris, Billingsgate, London
Grant and May, Billingsgate, London
Neunes, Billingsgate, London
Johnny Noble, Loch Fyne Oysters, Ardkinglass
Jeremy McCay, Bon Appetit, Ripley
Roy Stubbs, Smithfield, London
Simon Loftus, Adnams of Southwold
Christian Petrossian, Petrossian, Paris
Odette De Lalagrande, Maison de Caviar, Paris
Neville Abraham and Laurence Isaacson, Café Fish, London
Martin Palmer, Pyrmont Fish Market, Sydney
Carolyn Lockhart, Vogue Australia, Sydney
Wendy Huggard, Sydney Hilton, Sydney
New South Wales Sea Fish Authority
Terri O'Hara, Massachussets Division of Marine Fisheries, Massachusetts
Norway Sardine Industry, San Francisco
Len Porter, Simon Dickie Adventures, Taupo
Helen Gardiner, The Cascades, Taupo
Julia Vickerman, The Regent, Auckland
Garry Court, Air New Zealand
Chris Weber, Sky Courier International
Cliff Brooks, Konica Ubix
Mary Loring, Sphere Books Ltd

Chefs and Restaurants:

U.K.

Stewart Bassett, Old Rectory, Campsea Ash; Whiting Terrine

Raymond Blanc, Les Quatres Saison, Oxford; Smoked Haddock
    Tartare

Adrian Clarke, The Famous Fox and Goose, Fressingfield; Grilled
    Mussels

Dominique Cure, The Bleeding Heart, London; Soupe de Poissons,
    Sole with Lemongrass.

Charles Fontaine, Caprice, London; Salmon Cakes

Gerd Jacobmeyer, The Restaurant, Sheraton Park Tower; Seafood
    Timbale in Muscadet Jelly

Nico Ladenis, Simply Nico, London; Sea Bass en Croûte

Alistair Little, Alistair Little, London; Cuttlefish in Ink Sauce

Tim Reeson, The Crown, Southwold; Marinated Sea Bass

Brian Turner, Turner's Restaurant, London; Marinated Scallops

L'Escargot; Sardines in Sea Salt

Gino, San Lorenzo, London; Bagna Cauda

Savoy Hotel, London; Omelette Arnold Bennet

Luciano, Ziani's, London; Seafood Risotto

Italy

Villa San Michele, Fiesole, Florence; Red Snapper and Walnut
    Salad

Giannino's, San Remo; Marinated Lobster

U.S.A.

Le Bernadin, New York; Tuna Carpaccio

Casual Quilted Giraffe, New York; Lobster in Vanilla Bean Salad

Oyster Bar, Grand Central Station, New York; Skate Salad in
    Tarragon Vinaigrette

Ken Frank, La Toque, Los Angeles; Swordfish in Black Olive
    Sauce

Wolfgang Puck, Spago, Los Angeles; Grilled Tuna in Tomato and
    Basil Vinaigrette

Olde Porte Inn, Avila Beach, California; Cioppino

Legal Seafoods, Boston; Blackened Mackerel

Mexico
Villa Vera Racquet Club, Acapulco; Ceviche

Tahiti
Tahiti Beachcomber, Papeete; Kokoda-Poisson Cru

South Africa
Michael Arlt, The Beverley Hills Hotel, Umhlanga Rocks, Natal;
    Peri-Peri Sauce

New Zealand
Serafin Bueno, The Regent, Auckland; John Dory in Raspberry
    Viniagrette, Prawns on Potato Basil Purée in Champagne
    Vinaigrette
Greg Heffernan, Huka Lodge, Taupo; Gravlax, Trout and Brown
    Sugar

Australia
Andrew Blake, Chez Oz, Sydney; Oysters in Champagne
Richard Bullock, Chloe's, Sydney; Squid and Sesame Salad
Serge Dansereau, Kables, The Regent, Sydney; Roasted Mussels in
    Sake
Peter Doyle, Reflections, Sydney; Prawns in Orange Butter Sauce
Yves Meraud, San Francisco Grill, Hilton, Sydney; Scallops on
    Lettuce Coulis
Anders Ousbach, The Wharf, Sydney; Sea Bream with Chive and
    Basil Butter
Neil Perry, Blue Waters Grill, Sydney; Stuffed Charcoal Grilled
    Squid

BIBLIOGRAPHY

References, Recipe Sources and Further Reading

Ackart, Robert, *Frugal Fish Cookbook* (Little, Brown and Co., 1983)

Aitcheson, Carole Conde, *NZ Trout and Salmon Cookbook* (Reed Methuen Publishers Ltd, 1985)

Beadell, Suzanne, *The Complete Angler's Wife* (Country Wise Books, 1964)

Bissell, Frances, *A Cook's Calendar* (Chatto and Windus, Ltd, 1985)

Bocuse, Paul, *Poissons et Viandes* (Flammarion, 1984)

California Culinary Academy, *Fish and Shellfish* (Ortho Information, 1985)

Carlier, Alexandra, *Dinner Party Cookbook*

Carrier, Robert, *Great Dishes of the World* (Sphere Books Ltd, 1964)

Christian, Glyn, *Delicatessen Cook Book* (Macdonald and Co. Ltd, 1984)

Davidson, Alan, *Mediterranean Seafood* (Penguin Books Ltd, 1972)

Davidson, Alan, *North Atlantic Seafood* (Macmillan Publishers Ltd, 1979)

Faria, Susan, *The Northeast Seafood Book* (Mass. Division Marine Fisheries, 1984)

Floyd, Keith, *Floyd on Fish* (BBC Books, 1985)

Franey, Pierre and Miller, Bryan, *The Seafood Cookbook* (Times Books Ltd, 1986)

Grigson, Jane, *Fish Cookery* (Penguin Books, 1975)

Guerard, Michel, *Cuisine Minceur* (Macmillan Publishers Ltd, 1977)

Heath, Ambrose, *Madame Prunier's Fish Cookery* (Hurst and Blackett, 1938)

Hemphill, Rosemary, *Book of Herbs and Spices* (Omega Books Ltd, 1984)

Hicks, Susan, *Seafish Cookbook* (Hamlyn, 1986)

Horsley, Janet, *The New Fish Cookbook* (Macdonald and Co. Ltd, 1986)

Jaine, Tom, *Cooking in the Country* (Chatto and Windus Ltd, 1987)

Ladenis, Nico, *My Gastronomy* (Ebury Press, 1987)

Lale-Demoz, Jean-Jacques, *Jean-Jacques Seafood* (Nelson & Sons Ltd)

Lassalle, George, *Adventurous Fish Cook* (Macmillan Publishers Ltd, 1976)

Law, Digby, *The Entree Cookbook* (Lindon Publishing, 1984)

Lockhart, Carolyn (ed.), *Entertaining Guides* (Vogue Australia)

Lyon, Ninette and Barton, Maggie, *Fish For All Seasons* (Faber and Faber Ltd, 1966)

MacAndrew, Ian, *A Feast of Fish* (Macdonald, Orbis, 1987)

McCance and Widderson, *Composition of Foods* (HMSO, 1978)

McVinnie, Ray, *NZ Fish Cookery* (Reed Methuen Publishers Ltd, 1986)

Margittai, Tom and Kovi, Paul, *Four Seasons Cookbook* (Fireside Books, 1980)

Maschler, Fay, and Howard, Elizabeth Jane, *Food* (Michael Joseph Ltd, 1987)

Miller, Peter and Nicholls, James, *Guide to the Fishes of Great Britain* (Treasure Press, 1980)

Montagne, Prosper, *Larousse Gastronomique* (Hamlyn, 1977)

Mosiman, Anton, *Cuisine Naturelle* (Macmillan Publishers Ltd, 1985)

Mosiman, Anton, and Hoffman, Holger, *Shellfish* (Hamlyn, 1987)

Nathan, *Poissons et Fruits de Mer*

Pederson, Elizabeth, *NZ Seafood Cookery* (Wilson and Horton Ltd, 1986)

Pepin, Jacques, *La Technique et La Methode* (Methuen London Ltd, 1979)

Piccinardi, Antonio, *La Bonne Cuisine de la Mer* (Solar Press)

Puck, Wolfgang, *Wolfgang Puck Cookbook* (Random House Inc., 1986)

Reige, Odette, *Les Poissons* (Hubschmidt et Bowet, 1984)

Root, Waverley, *Food* (Simon and Schuster)

Simms, A. E., *Fish and Shellfish in the International Cuisine* (Virtue and Co., Ltd, 1973)

Smith, R. G., *Poissons, Coquillage et Crustaces* (Grund Librairie, 1986)

Spear, Ruth, *Cooking Fish and Shellfish* (Ballantine, 1984)

Spencer, Colin, *Fish Cookbook* (Pan Books Ltd, 1986)

Verger, Roger, *Cuisine of the Sun* (Macmillan Books Ltd)

Williams, Anne, *F for Fish* (Dent and Sons Ltd, 1987)

Worthington, Diane R., *California Cuisine* (Tarcher Inc., 1983)

Daily Mail, London
Evening Standard, London
Los Angeles Times, Los Angeles
N3 News, Boston, Massachusetts
New England Medical Journal, Massachusetts
New York Times, New York
Seafood Business Report, Camden, Maine
The Times, London